Abraham Lincoln

16th President of the United States

Abraham Lincoln, the President who guided the United States through the tragedy of its only civil war and who abolished slavery, was at times one of the nation's most unpopular Presidents. Yet today his image is instantly recognized around the world as an honored and beloved symbol of America. (Library of Congress.)

Abraham Lincoln
16th President of the United States

Rebecca Stefoff

 GARRETT EDUCATIONAL CORPORATION

Cover: *Official presidential portrait of Abraham Lincoln by George P.A. Healy.* (Copyrighted by the White House Historical Association; photograph by the National Geographic Society.)

1999 Printing

Manufactured in the United States of America

Edited and produced by Synthegraphics Corporation

Library of Congress Cataloging in Publication Data

Stefoff, Rebecca, 1951–
   Abraham Lincoln, 16th president of the United States.

   (Presidents of the United States)
   Bibliography: p.
   Includes index.
   Summary: Surveys the childhood, education, employment, and political career of the Civil War president.
   1. Lincoln, Abraham, 1809–1865 — Juvenile literature.
2. Presidents — United States — Biography — Juvenile literature. [1. Lincoln, Abraham, 1809–1865. 2. Presidents] I. Title. II. Title: Abraham Lincoln, sixteenth president of the United States. III. Series.
E457.905.S69   1989   973.7092/4   [B] [92]   88-28488
ISBN 0-944483-14-3

Contents

Chronology for
Abraham Lincoln

1809 Born on February 12 in Hardin County, Kentucky

1816 Moved to Indiana with family

1830 Moved to Illinois with family

1832 Served as captain of Illinois militia in Indian wars

1834–
1842 Served for four terms in Illinois state legislature

1842 Married Mary Ann Todd on November 4 in Springfield, Illinois

1847–
1849 Served for one term as a Whig congressman in the U.S. House of Representatives

1856 Joined the newly formed Republican Party

1860 Elected to first term as President of the United States

1861 Civil War started on April 12

1863 Signed the Emancipation Proclamation on January 1; delivered the Gettysburg Address on November 19

1864 Elected to second term as President

1865 Confederacy surrendered on April 9, ending the Civil War; Lincoln assassinated by John Wilkes Booth on April 14

Chapter 1

A New Birth of Freedom

On July 1, 1863, the hills and fields around the small Pennsylvania town of Gettysburg lay empty and baking under a hot midsummer sun. As noon approached, a haze of dust hung in the air, stirred up by thousands upon thousands of marching feet. Their steady tramp-tramp-tramp could be felt as a quiver in the earth underfoot.

Soon the air began to ring with the distant echoes of footsteps, hoofbeats, and shouts that grew closer moment by moment. Two great armies were converging on Gettysburg, one from the southeast and one from the west. They met before noon, just south of town, and the battle that they fought there was the bloodiest — and probably the most famous — in American history. It was also the turning point of the American Civil War.

Approaching from the west was the Army of the Confederacy, as the southern states that had seceded (withdrawn) from the United States called themselves. It numbered about 75,000 soldiers and was led by General Robert E. Lee, perhaps the best military commander of his time. After two years of fighting in the South, Lee was carrying the war to the North by invading the Union state of Pennsylvania. He marched his men, in their threadbare gray uniforms, toward Gettysburg because he had heard that the town had a large supply of shoes, which the Confederate army desperately needed.

Advancing on the town from the southeast was the Union, or northern, army with close to 101,000 men, of whom about 84,000 were in prime fighting shape. The Union army was called the Army of the Potomac; it was led by General George G. Meade, who had taken command just days before.

In late June, Meade and the Union army were in Frederick, Maryland, when he received word of Lee's advance into Pennsylvania. Under orders from President Abraham Lincoln to halt Lee's drive into the North and to crush the Confederate army, Meade rushed to intercept Lee. If the South could be decisively defeated on the battlefield, Lincoln believed, it would have to rejoin the Union—and the United States would be whole again.

A THREE-DAY ORDEAL

The forward troops of the two armies clashed at about noon. Armed with recently invented repeating rifles, the Union troops were able to hold the attacking Confederates at bay. Nevertheless, by the end of the day, the Confederates had inflicted heavy losses on the Union forces. But Meade's troops were now dug in behind stone walls on the top of a long hill called Cemetery Ridge, which gave them a good defensive position.

During the second day of the battle, desperate fighting took place below Cemetery Ridge on level ground to the west. A peach orchard, a wheat field, and a small hollow called Devil's Den were soon drenched with the blood of soldiers of both sides. By day's end, Union forces had captured two hills, Round Top and Little Round Top. And the Confederate army was now positioned atop a long hill called Seminary Ridge, which ran parallel to and about 1,400 yards west of Cemetery Ridge. The Confederates had received the worst of the fighting, and one of their generals, J. B. Hood, was seriously wounded.

The third day was even more grim. By now, both armies were exhausted and suffering from crippling losses. The dead littered the open ground between Seminary Ridge and Cemetery Ridge. Wounded men lay where they had fallen, crying out for water, but there were not nearly enough medical supplies or attendants to care for all of them. Under fire from the enemy above, neither army stood a good chance of crossing the open ground between the two ridges and mounting a successful assault on the opposite ridge. Nevertheless, Lee decided to attack again.

The Confederate attack began with a barrage of artillery fire aimed at the Union troops on Cemetery Ridge, but most of it went over their heads. Then, in mid-afternoon, the Union soldiers watched in awed silence as fully 15,000 Confederate men marched toward them across the deadly stretch of clear ground that separated the two ridges. But the silence was soon broken. When the Confederates had covered about half the distance to Cemetery Ridge, the Union forces opened fire with their own thundering cannon. The effect was devastating.

Pickett's Charge

The Union barrage immediately thinned the Confederate ranks, mowing down rows upon rows of men as if with a sickle. Some southerners, however, made it through the hail of artillery shells, only to face the rifle fire of 10,000 northern infantrymen.

One spearhead of the Confederate advance — 4,500 men of General G. E. Pickett's divison — did succeed in reaching

Cemetery Ridge. But Pickett's Charge, as this action was later called, was a gallant but doomed effort. Under attack from three sides and gravely weakened by the artillery onslaught, Pickett's men were forced to retreat, leaving their battle-torn flags behind. Three-quarters of the 4,500 men were either killed or wounded. Pickett's Charge has been called "the high tide of the Confederacy" because, after its failure, the tide of war turned against the South.

Pickett's Charge was also the last action of the Battle of Gettysburg. The battered remnants of the Confederate army retreated to Seminary Ridge as evening fell. There Lee waited through the long night and the next day, dreading a Union attack. But because the Army of the Potomac had also suffered extensive losses in the three days of fighting, Meade did not attack. Then, on the night of July 4, in a heavy downpour of rain, the demoralized Confederate army began its retreat to Virginia. The long, dreadful battle was over.

The Cost of Gettysburg

In terms of human life, the Battle of Gettysburg was the costliest military encounter in American history. More than 28,000 Confederate and more than 23,000 Union soldiers were killed or injured. Despite these staggering losses, neither side could truly claim a victory. Meade did succeed in halting the Confederate advance into the North, but he failed to destroy Lee's army, which lived to fight another day. Lee, in turn, was unable to hold his ground in Pennsylvania, and his army never recovered its strength.

The Battle of Gettysburg was costly in political terms, too. People on both sides were shocked and horrified by the casualty reports. In the South, Confederate leaders began an agonizing analysis of the encounter, alternately criticizing and praising Lee and his fellow generals, endlessly refighting the battle and trying to find out just where the South went wrong.

In the North, the death toll added strength to a growing anti-war movement that attacked President Lincoln and his conduct of the war. In the meantime, Lincoln was furious that Meade, instead of following and attacking the reeling southerners, had allowed Lee's army to retreat. "We had them within our grasp," the President cried. "We had only to stretch forth our hands and they were ours." But one of the most memorable and far-reaching effects of the battle was yet to come.

A SPEECH AT GETTYSBURG

After the Battle of Gettysburg, the battlefield was a terrible sight, littered with the bodies of thousands of men and horses. Because it was impossible to return all of the dead soldiers to their homes for burial, they were buried on the spot. A Gettysburg attorney named David Wills then proposed that the battlefield be dedicated as a National Soldier's Cemetery. After the state governor approved the plan, a dedication ceremony was scheduled for November 19, 1863. Edward Everett, a famous preacher, statesman, and orator from Boston, was to be the main speaker. The organizers of the event also invited President Lincoln to make "a few appropriate remarks."

During his three years as President, Lincoln had turned down many such requests and invitations. The war and the demands of his office kept him busy to the point of exhaustion, and he felt he could not spare the time from his vital duties for public appearances. Now, however, Lincoln felt that it was time for a statement about why the North was fighting the war, and why it was necessary above all else to preserve the Union. So he accepted the invitation to speak at Gettysburg.

President Lincoln's short speech at Gettysburg, captured in this picture by painter Fletcher C. Ransom, was delivered in sight of the fields where more than 50,000 men were killed or wounded in the bloodiest battle of the Civil War. The speech was a simple and heartfelt plea for the preservation of the Union—even at such a terrible cost. (Library of Congress.)

A Lincoln Legend

Many legends have grown up around Lincoln over the years. One of the most enduring of these legends says that he hastily scribbled his Gettysburg Address on the back of an envelope during the train ride to Gettysburg. Like many other Lincoln legends, this often-told tale is untrue.

Lincoln started working on his Gettysburg speech before he left Washington. But by the time he boarded the special train bound for Gettysburg on November 18, the speech was still not finished. The President confided to his friend Noah Brooks that it would be "short, short, short."

Perhaps Lincoln had hoped to finish his speech on the train, but he found himself unable to work. The train was crowded with Washington notables and loud with conversation. Lincoln was drawn into a lively political discussion among his two private secretaries and several of his Cabinet members. In the few quiet moments, he worried about his young son Tad, who was sick with a fever. The unfinished speech remained in his pocket.

Gettysburg was packed with people who had come for the dedication ceremony. Many of them were relatives of Union soldiers who had died on the battlefield. Lincoln, his Cabinet members, and orator Everett made their way through the crowded streets to Wills' house, where they were to dine and spend the night. There, an elegant, formal dinner was followed by serenades of band music as crowds outside the Wills home cheered Lincoln.

Before he went upstairs to the guest bedroom, Lincoln was handed a telegram from Secretary of War Edwin Stanton. "All is quiet on the battlefronts," Stanton reported, and went on to add, "Mrs. Lincoln informs me that your son is better this evening." Cheered by this news, Lincoln sat up late into the night, finishing his speech and writing it out on two sheets of paper. He added a few final touches early the next morning, which dawned with rain.

Two Immortal Minutes

After breakfast, the dedication party set out for the battlefield in a long, slow procession. Soldiers saluted, guns were fired, and flags flew at half-mast in mourning. As they marched, the clouds melted away and the sun shone brightly from a clear autumn sky. When the procession reached the top of Cemetery Ridge, the speakers mounted a low wooden platform, while the audience—between 15,000 and 20,000 people—milled about below them.

Everett spoke first. He talked for two hours, describing the battle and comparing the American Civil War with episodes in European history. His speech was polished and professional, delivered with all the gestures and speaking skills of a practiced orator. After a time, though, some people in the audience grew restless and began to drift away to see the sights of the battlefield. From where he sat on the speakers' platform, Lincoln also studied the panorama.

He could see Seminary Ridge, where Lee's army had dug in, less than a mile to the west. Nearer at hand were the peach orchard and the wheat field where some of the fiercest fighting had occurred. Round Top and Little Round Top, site of Pickett's desperate charge, were on his left. In the distance, the gentle mountains of central Pennsylvania rose in a hazy blue wall. All around, the trees glowed with the reds and golds of autumn.

But the serenity of the scene was marred by evidence of man's presence: rows upon rows of shallow Union graves, each with its wooden marker; shattered tree limbs and gaping holes in the earth torn by artillery shells; the skeletons of cavalry horses lying in the tall grass; and the mounds of rocks where Confederate soldiers had been buried in the little hollow called Devil's Den. Perhaps, as he sat there during Everett's speech, Lincoln imagined for a moment that his sight was darkened by the dust and smoke of battle, and that his ears rang with gunfire, the cries of the wounded, and the shrill neighing of frightened horses.

At last, Everett took his seat. Lincoln rose, put on his spectacles, and took the two sheets of paper from his pocket.

He walked to the front of the platform and said, "Four score and seven years ago our fathers brought forth on this continent, a new nation, conceived in Liberty, and dedicated to the proposition that all men are created equal."

Lincoln spoke in his characteristically high-pitched, penetrating voice for about two minutes. It is said that a photographer in the audience, intending to take a picture of the President delivering his speech, started to set up his camera— but by the time he was ready to take the picture, Lincoln had finished speaking. The speech was only 10 sentences long. Its message was a reminder of what, in Lincoln's view, the Civil War was all about. The soldiers who died at Gettysburg gave their lives in a struggle that was testing the strength of the very foundation of America, the democratic union of the states. That union must not be allowed to fail, or these men and others would have died in vain.

Instead of attacking the South, Lincoln spoke only of the high ideals of democratic government and the hopes of the country's founding fathers. He called upon all the people to dedicate themselves anew to those ideals and hopes, so that "this nation, under God, shall have a new birth of freedom."

The crowd may have been surprised at the brevity of Lincoln's speech, but it cheered him loud and long. And then, as John Hay, one of the President's secretaries, wrote later, "the music wailed, and we went home through crowded and cheering streets." That night, a weary Lincoln returned to Washington by train.

Words that Wouldn't Die

Lincoln had done his best with the speech he gave at Gettysburg. He had struggled to capture in a few resounding sentences all that he deeply believed about America's meaning

Lincoln's Gettysburg Address

Four score and seven years ago our fathers brought forth on this continent, a new nation, conceived in Liberty, and dedicated to the proposition that all men are created equal.

Now we are engaged in a great civil war, testing whether that nation or any nation so conceived and so dedicated can long endure. We are met on a great battlefield of that war. We have come to dedicate a portion of that field, as a final resting place for those who here gave their lives that that nation might live. It is altogether fitting and proper that we should do this.

But, in a larger sense, we can not dedicate — we can not consecrate — we can not hallow — this ground. The brave men, living and dead, who struggled here, have consecrated it far above our poor power to add or detract. The world will little note, nor long remember what we say here, but it can never forget what they did here. It is for us the living, rather, to be dedicated here to the unfinished work which they who fought here have thus far so nobly advanced. It is rather for us to be here dedicated to the great task remaining before us — that from these honored dead we take increased devotion to that cause for which they gave the last full measure of devotion — that we here highly resolve that these dead shall not have died in vain — that this nation, under God, shall have a new birth of freedom — and that government of the people, by the people, for the people, shall not perish from the earth.

in the world, its destiny, and the duties of its people. Afterward, though, he felt that his Gettysburg speech was a failure. Perhaps it was too short, too simple, too different from the flowery, long-drawn-out style that was favored by public speakers of the time. This opinion was shared by some newspaper writers, who criticized the President's speech, saying it was not grand enough for such an important occasion. Some papers printed Everett's entire speech and didn't even mention Lincoln's.

But Lincoln's speech at Gettysburg was not forgotten. Its plain and direct language, its impassioned reminder of democratic principles, and its hopeful call for national brotherhood were too powerful to be forgotten. As the memory of Everett's oration faded, people remembered Lincoln's speech and quoted from it, and it gradually entered the minds and hearts of the nation.

Lincoln himself wrote out six copies of the Gettysburg Address, as it came to be known. Five of them survive, with minor variations in wording and punctuation but with the clear thinking and deep feeling of a great mind visible in every line. As he penned these pages, which are now national treasures, the President did not dream that his words would be memorized by schoolchildren in generations to come. He could not have imagined that one day they would be carved into a majestic marble slab in the United States capital, where each year hundreds of thousands of people from every part of the world would come to read or hear what Abraham Lincoln said that long-ago November day in a small Pennsylvania town.

In his speech, Lincoln said, "The world will little note, nor long remember what we say here." He was wrong. His words have been long remembered.

Chapter 2

Frontier Boyhood

A braham Lincoln's face, once seen, could never be forgotten. Gaunt and harsh-featured, fringed with a dark beard, topped with unruly hair and a tall stovepipe hat, Lincoln's face has become one of the most familiar and recognizable symbols of America. But what was the man behind this symbol really like?

Lincoln's private and public selves were made up of contradictions. He was known for his sharp wit, his ready good humor, and his love of jokes, anecdotes, and story-telling. Yet he could be melancholy as well as mirthful, and he suffered through many periods of dark, troublesome depression.

His countrymen loved to think of Lincoln as Honest Abe, the ax-swinging, log-splitting frontier boy who grew up to be President. But Lincoln had no love for the poverty and emptiness of frontier life; he escaped from it as soon as he could. Long before he became President, Lincoln was a wealthy and successful businessman. He also hated the nickname "Abe," preferring to be called "Lincoln."

However, traces of the frontier remained with Lincoln all his life. His speech was that of the backwoods and prairie: he said *kin* for "can," *cheer* for "chair," and *haint* for "haven't." By his own estimation, he attended less than a year's worth of school in his whole life. Yet he was a skilled and knowledgeable lawyer who loved to quote poetry and discuss the meaning of Shakespeare's plays.

The biggest contradictions of Lincoln's life centered on the national tragedy of the Civil War. He became President at a time when sectionalism, or rivalry between different sections of the nation, was tearing the United States apart. His task was to hold the country together. To do so, he had to search for compromises.

Although Lincoln hated slavery, he tried for a long time to keep the southern slave states happy. This made those northerners who wanted to stamp out slavery angry with him. On the other hand, although he did not fight the Civil War in order to end slavery, he went down in history as the Great Emancipator—the man who freed the slaves. This made many southerners hate and fear him. And although Lincoln was a man who deeply wanted to believe that people's lives should be governed by justice, logic, and reason, he was driven by circumstances to fight the country's bloodiest, most agonizing war.

The challenges that Lincoln faced as President were perhaps greater than those confronted by any other President before him—yet somehow he found the strength and the skill to meet them. Frederick Douglass, the black leader of the anti-slavery movement of Lincoln's day, said that "infinite wisdom has seldom sent any man into the world better fitted for his mission than Abraham Lincoln." And Carl Sandburg, an American poet of the 20th century who wrote a six-volume life of Lincoln, recognized the rare combination of the stern and the compassionate in Lincoln when he said, "Not often in the story of mankind does a man arrive on earth who is both steel and velvet, who is hard as rock and soft as drifting fog."

QUAKER ROOTS

The earliest of Lincoln's ancestors known in the New World was Samuel Lincoln, an apprentice weaver who came to the Massachusetts Bay Colony from Norfolk, England, in about 1637. His descendants carried the Lincoln name and family into New Jersey, Pennsylvania, and Virginia. The early American Lincolns were Quakers, members of William Penn's Society of Friends, but later generations no longer professed Quaker beliefs.

Lincoln's paternal grandfather, who was also named Abraham Lincoln, fought in the American Revolution as a captain in the Virginia militia. One of his friends was frontiersman Daniel Boone, who told Lincoln that land could be had cheaply in Kentucky. So, in 1782, Lincoln moved his family to Jefferson County, east of Louisville, Kentucky. There he worked to carve out a homestead from the wilderness. Four years later, while planting a field of corn, he was killed by an Indian.

Father and Mother

Grandfather Abraham's son Thomas was eight years old when his father was killed. He became a hard-working farmer and carpenter, served in the Kentucky militia, and in 1806 married Nancy Hanks. Little is known about Nancy Hanks Lincoln's background. Although she met Thomas Lincoln while she was staying with friends or relatives in Washington County, Kentucky, she was born in Virginia. It is possible that she was an illegitimate child; at any rate, she seems never to have spoken about her parents.

Thomas Lincoln and his bride settled near Hodgenville,

in Hardin County, Kentucky (now called Larue County). There, in a one-room cabin with a dirt floor and a single window, their daughter Nancy was born in 1807; they gave her the nickname Sarah. Two years later, on February 12, 1809, a son was born. They named him Abraham, after Thomas' father. A third child, Thomas, was born in 1811 but died in infancy, as did many children of that time and place—doctors and medicine were scarce and life was hard.

When Abraham was about two years old, his father moved the family to a new homestead about 10 miles away. The cabin where Lincoln was born soon rotted away or was torn down. Today a replica stands on the original homestead, which is called Sinking Spring Farm.

The Lincolns' new home, a 230-acre farm on Knob Creek, was the site of Abraham's earliest memories: his father planting pumpkin seeds between rows of corn; later, a flash flood washing away the laboriously planted corn and pumpkin seeds; another time, slipping down a muddy bank into the swirling creek and floundering there half-drowned until a neighbor boy pulled him out.

Knob Creek was also the place where Abraham had his first schooling. In the winter of 1815, and again in 1816, he and Sarah were spared for a few weeks or months from their chores so they could attend school. Frontier schoolhouses of the period were usually one-room log cabins. They were called "blab schools" because the pupils of all ages sat around the room and recited their lessons out loud. The schools were opened whenever a preacher, lawyer, or anyone with a shred of education was available to teach for a while. All his life Lincoln remembered the names of Zacariah Riney and Caleb Hazel, the teachers who taught him the basics of reading and writing during those two brief school sessions.

North to Indiana

In December of 1816, Thomas Lincoln moved his family again. A legal dispute had arisen over the ownership of the Knob Creek land, and he decided to start over somewhere else. The Lincolns loaded their possessions onto two horses and set out on a 100-mile journey to Spencer County in southwestern Indiana. They crossed the Ohio River and made their way through muddy forests and thorny undergrowth to the Little Pigeon Creek area. Abraham, who was seven, long remembered this trip as the most grueling experience of his life.

At Little Pigeon Creek, Thomas Lincoln and his son quickly threw together a "half-faced camp," a crude shelter of logs and branches with one side open to the weather. They had to keep the fire burning constantly—for warmth and for protection against wild animals. Huddled around the fire, Abraham heard wolves howl and wildcats scream in the darkness. Bears carried off some of the family's pigs.

When the ground thawed in the spring, Thomas and Abraham began work on a new cabin. Eight years old by now, Abraham was lean and long-limbed, "a tall spider of a boy," as one neighbor remembered. He helped his father chop down trees to clear the land on which they built a 360-square-foot log cabin, larger than the one at Knob Creek. Like the Knob Creek homestead, this cabin consisted of a single room, but it had a loft. At night, Abraham climbed up a ladder and slept in the low-ceilinged loft.

LINCOLN GROWS UP

It was a good thing that Thomas and Abraham had built a larger cabin. Soon after it was finished, Thomas and Elizabeth Sparrow, relatives of Nancy, came to live with the Lincolns.

With them came Dennis Hanks, the son of one of Nancy's aunts. Although Dennis was 10 years older than Abraham, the two boys became friends, sharing the chores and wrestling and running together.

A year later, in the summer of 1818, southern Indiana was ravaged by an epidemic of disease. The epidemic took the lives of the Sparrows and then, in October, it took Nancy Hanks Lincoln's life as well. Thomas Lincoln made his wife's coffin, and Abraham never forgot whittling the wooden pegs that held the coffin together. His mother was buried in an unmarked grave on a barren nearby hill.

That winter was a bleak, lonely time. Lincoln missed his mother, whom he always remembered with affection. Although she could not read and had to sign documents with a shaky "X," she was deeply religious and loved to tell her children Bible stories she had learned by heart.

Lincoln seldom spoke of his mother in later years, mentioning only that she was affectionate and sad-faced, and that the harsh life of the frontier had made her look old beyond her years. But he remembered that she had encouraged him to take advantage of his few chances to attend school, and that she had worked hard and hoped for a better life for her children. "All that I am or hope to be," he once said, "I owe to my sainted mother."

A New Family

A year after Nancy Lincoln's death, Abraham's father made a journey to Kentucky and returned home with a new wife. Her name was Sarah Bush Johnston, although everyone called her Sally; she was a widow with three children. She took to Abraham and Sarah Lincoln at once, and they to her. She became, as Abraham later put it, "a good and kind mother" to the motherless Lincolns.

With Dennis Hanks and the three Johnston children, the cabin was now home to eight people. But Thomas and the boys spent a great deal of time out of doors, busy with the hundreds of chores of a frontier farm. Even as a youngster, Lincoln was tall, with wiry but strong muscles. Unlike most frontier boys, he didn't like hunting and fishing, but he gained great skill with an ax. He not only cut down trees, chopped firewood, and split fence rails for his father, but was hired out to work on neighboring farms at the rate of 25 cents a day, payable to Thomas Lincoln. Abraham also mastered the arts of guiding a horse-drawn plow and of harvesting corn and other crops. During these years, however, his distaste for the rugged frontier life was growing — and along with it grew his thirst for knowledge and for the larger world that lay beyond the homestead.

A Backwoods Bookworm

Abraham hadn't forgotten the scraps of learning he had picked up at the blab school that he and Sarah had attended in Kentucky. In Spencer County he added to his learning "by littles," as he later said, with occasional lessons from schoolteachers named Andrew Crawford, James Swaney, and Azel Dorsey. Lincoln loved to read, and he always found ways to snatch moments for reading from the dawn-to-dusk grind of farm labor. When he was plowing a field, for example, he carried a book and read a page or two at the end of each row, while the horses rested. "I never saw Abe after he was twelve that he didn't have a book in his hand or in his pocket," Dennis Hanks later marvelled. "It didn't seem natural to see a feller read like that."

Because books were scarce in the backwoods community, each was precious. Abraham would walk for miles to borrow a book and would read it over and over again. He read the family Bible from cover to cover several times, but his favorites were colorful and exciting tales like *Robinson Crusoe* and *The Arabian Nights*. He loved the dry, homey humor of *Aesop's Fables*, which had animal characters that seemed familiar to a country boy. And he also liked *Pilgrim's Progress*, a classic English sermon on morals disguised as a tale.

But Lincoln's favorite book was a biography of George Washington by Parson Weems, who was responsible for starting many of the stories about Washington that are now known to be fictional, such as the incident with the hatchet and the cherry tree. Abraham thrilled to Weems' stirring accounts of the birth of the United States and the heroism of its founding fathers. His profound admiration for Washington and Thomas Jefferson dates from this childhood reading.

Lincoln practiced his writing, too, embellishing one page of careful schoolwork with a poem that is the earliest piece of his handwriting known to survive:

> Abraham Lincoln
> his hand and pen
> he will be good but
> god knows When.

Later he sharpened his writing skills with more poetry, but it has been lost.

Abraham also loved making speeches to his friends from doorsteps and tree stumps — he didn't know it at the time, but this was good practice for the politician he would someday become. He sometimes imitated the lively orations of the roving preachers and revivalists who held religious meetings in frontier communities.

As far as his own religious beliefs were concerned, Abraham never belonged to an organized church, although he believed in God. Thomas and Sally Lincoln joined the Pigeon

$100 REWARD!

RANAWAY

From the undersigned, living on Current River, about twelve miles above Doniphan,

in Ripley County, Mo., on 2nd of March, 1860, A NEGRO MAN, about 30 years old, weighs about 160 pounds; high forehead, with a scar on it; had on brown pants and coat very much worn, and an old black wool hat; shoes size No. 11.

The above reward will be given to any person who may apprehend this said negro out of the State; and fifty dollars if apprehended in this State outside of Ripley county, or $25 if taken in Ripley county.

APOS TUCKER.

This poster, offering a reward for the return of a runaway slave, is dated 1860, but such posters were common sights during Lincoln's youth. His father and stepmother belonged to a church that preached against slavery, and he probably was influenced by their beliefs. (Library of Congress.)

Creek Baptist Church, whose preacher was famous for his sermons against slavery. Abraham probably heard and agreed with some of these sermons, but he did not join the church.

Flatboat to New Orleans

At age 17, Abraham began to find occasional work on Ohio River ferryboats. He had a skiff, or small open boat, of his own that he sometimes used to carry passengers ashore from the large steamboats that had begun to ply the river. And in the spring of 1828, when he was just 19, he had a chance for a real river adventure.

Abraham's sister, Sarah, had just died in childbirth. Lincoln grieved for her, but her death seemed to loosen one of the ties that bound him to his home and family. He became increasingly impatient to start out on his own and see something of the world. When James Gentry, a well-to-do local merchant, offered him a job taking a flatboat-load of farm produce to New Orleans, he jumped at the chance.

Together with Gentry's son Allen, Abraham set off in April on the 1,200-mile journey down the Ohio River to the Mississippi River, and then down the Mississippi to the bustling port of New Orleans. The great river must have appeared to the two young men much as it was portrayed a few years later by another Midwesterner, Mark Twain.

In his books *Life on the Mississippi* and *The Adventures of Huckleberry Finn*, Twain describes the river as treacherous with shifting currents and snags, busy with traffic of all sizes from skiffs to paddle-wheel steamboats, and full of fascinating life and commerce. In the southern reaches of the river, the bluffs and forests along the banks gave way to exotic swamps and bayous, where the trees were hung with Spanish moss and brightly colored birds flitted through the foliage.

If the river journey was exciting, New Orleans was a glimpse of a whole new world. More than a thousand flatboats were tied up at its docks, and its harbor was crowded with tall-masted ships from all over the world. Sailors and travelers in the streets spoke many languages, creating a strange-sounding background noise. The high, narrow, painted houses of the French Quarter, with their delicate wrought-iron balconies, were as different as could be imagined from the cabins of Little Pigeon Creek.

One of the strangest and most uncomfortable sights in New Orleans was the slave market. Black men and women were auctioned there and led off in chains. With 200 or more slave dealers, New Orleans was a thriving center of the slave trade. Abraham spoke long afterward of the painful impression made on him by the sight of so many slaves and their obvious unhappiness.

After Abraham and Allen sold their produce, they made their way back up the Mississippi and Ohio rivers to Rockport, the village on the Ohio River from which they had started out three months earlier. There Abraham went inland to Little Pigeon Creek. He gave his wages — about $24 — to Thomas Lincoln; according to the laws and customs of the time, a son's earnings belonged to his father until the son was 21 years old and independent.

The Prairie Beckons

Abraham turned 21 in 1830. He could now go anywhere and do anything he wanted. He had long dreamed of escaping from the stifling drudgery of Little Pigeon Creek — and now, he discovered, his father was planning to leave also.

Thomas Lincoln had heard from John Hanks, one of Nancy's cousins who had settled in Illinois. John sent word that the rich topsoil of the Illinois prairie was infinitely easier to farm than the gnarled forestland of southern Indiana. Although Thomas Lincoln and his family had a comfortable life in Indiana, they decided to move west to the prairie.

Abraham decided to go with them. He was not yet sure just what he intended to do with his life, and he was curious about what Illinois might have to offer. Besides, his family needed his help one more time. He drove one of their ox-drawn wagons to a new settlement, which was located on the Sangamon River in central Illinois, west of Decatur. There, on the wide and windy prairie, Abraham helped his father and the others clear a few acres and build a cabin. Then winter set in.

John Hanks had not lied about the fertile farmland to be found in Illinois. Unfortunately, however, the Lincolns arrived at the beginning of one of the worst winters ever known in that region. First, everyone fell sick with the ague, an ailment accompanied by fevers and shaking. Then, in quick succession, a raging blizzard deposited several feet of snow, a freezing rain covered the snow with a thick coat of ice, and a bitter wind from the northwest held the temperature well below zero for nine weeks. More than once, no doubt, the Lincolns wished that they had stayed in Indiana.

When spring finally came, Abraham was ready with a plan. He had already made one flatboat trip to New Orleans. Why not make another? A local trader named Denton Offutt agreed to pay Abraham, John Hanks, and Abraham's step-brother, John Johnston, to take a load of goods downriver. As arranged, the three young men met Offutt in Springfield, Illinois, in March. His goods were ready for shipment. There was just one problem: he had somehow neglected to obtain a boat.

Abraham was determined to make his plan succeed. When Offutt suggested half-jokingly that they could build a boat, Abraham led the others to a spot on the riverbank and directed the fashioning of a crude but serviceable craft. The rest of the business went off without any further problems, and the three arrived back in Illinois several months later.

Offutt was impressed with Abraham's determination and offered him a job. The village of New Salem, on the Sanga-mon River, was a growing community that needed a general store, which Offutt planned to open. Because he also needed a clerk, he offered the job to Abraham with a salary of $15 a month and permission to sleep in the back of the store.

At last, Abraham had an opportunity to become indepen-dent without being a "hardscrabble" farmer like his father. He immediately accepted Offutt's offer with a thrill of excite-ment, but first, he wanted to make a quick visit to see his parents. During Abraham's last river trip to New Orleans, Thomas and Sally Lincoln had moved again, to a homestead in Coles County. Abraham wanted to be sure that they were settled in their new home and that they could get by without his help. After visiting his parents and seeing that they were all right, Abraham headed for New Salem, full of ambition and enthusiasm.

Chapter 3
The Self-Made Man

When Lincoln arrived in New Salem in the summer of 1831, he found a small, rough frontier village that was full of high hopes. Although there were only about 100 people in New Salem, the town was expected to grow once steamboat traffic reached the Sangamon River. In the meantime, it was a rather wild place, not all that different from Little Pigeon Creek, but it gave Lincoln the chance to live and work on his own.

THE NEWCOMER IN TOWN

Abraham later described himself as having been "friendless, uneducated, penniless" on his arrival in New Salem. Although he remained nearly penniless for some time, he quickly made friends and continued educating himself. By now, he was 22 years old. He was six feet, four inches tall, with long, gangly limbs and large, bony hands and feet. But his leanness was deceiving, for years of rail-splitting and other farm chores had given him boundless energy and astonishing strength. He was clean-shaven, with thick black hair, jutting eyebrows, and a prominent nose and ears. His eyes were his handsomest feature; they were a clear, luminous gray and sparkled with animation during conversation.

A Friend to All

Lincoln's first friendship in New Salem started out as a fight. Offutt had boasted that his new clerk was the best wrestler around, and this boast came to the attention of the village wrestling champion, a husky fellow named Jack Armstrong. He was the leader of a group of hard-drinking, rowdy young men called the Clary Grove Boys.

Armstrong challenged Lincoln to a wrestling match. When the two met, Lincoln started to get the better of Armstrong — until all of the Clary Grove Boys jumped on Lincoln. Angry but unafraid, the tall newcomer to town shouted that he would take them all on, but one at a time. Jack Armstrong was so impressed that he jumped up and shook Lincoln's hand, after which the two became good friends.

His friendship with the Clary Grove Boys might have made Lincoln look like just another ruffian to the more refined townspeople, but they soon discovered that he was something different. Although he spent time with the local rowdies, Lincoln didn't drink like they did. All his life, in fact, Abraham avoided liquor, saying that it made him feel "flabby and undone."

Lincoln's good humor and intelligence soon appealed to everyone who talked with him. He possessed the rare gifts of being interested in all sorts of people and of being able to be friends with everyone — from two-fisted riverboatmen to top-hatted doctors and lawyers.

A Thirst for Knowledge

Above all, Lincoln had not lost his thirst for knowledge. He got to know James Rutledge, a tavern owner who was one of the town's social leaders. Rutledge had a library of several dozen books that Lincoln read eagerly. Dr. John Allen, a Ver-

monter who had moved to New Salem, was the town's leading intellectual. He formed a weekly debating society that
met in Rutledge's tavern. One day Lincoln showed up at a
meeting of the society and asked permission to participate.
He made a speech in his high-pitched voice and surprised
the group with his logic and forcefulness. "He was already
a good speaker," Allen recalled later. "All he needed was some
culture."

Lincoln proceeded to acquire as much culture as he could
in the small frontier town. Mentor Graham, the local school-
master, liked Lincoln and gave him books to read. Lincoln
taught himself mathematics; indeed, Euclid's book on geom-
etry became one of his favorites. He also borrowed a gram-
mar book from Graham and studied it for months, polishing
his sentences. And he read Shakespeare over and over. Years
later, he was still able to recite large passages of *Hamlet* and
Macbeth by heart.

One other thing absorbed Lincoln's interest in the months
following his arrival in New Salem: politics. He could not
help but be impressed with the opportunities for advance-
ment and recognition that frontier politicians enjoyed. Many
successful politicians were self-made men from rustic back-
grounds, just like him. Lincoln was ambitious; he wanted to
find work that would be important, interesting, and well
respected. He also was genuinely interested in history, government, law, and political theory. He began to study the speeches
of visiting state politicians and party members and to debate
the national and local issues of the day.

WORK, WAR, AND POLITICS

In the meantime, Lincoln continued to work at Offutt's store,
until it failed in 1832. After looking around for a new line
of work, he decided to go into politics. He announced that

he would run for the Illinois state legislature in the fall. But before he could launch his campaign, a bulletin from Illinois Governor John Reynolds arrived in New Salem:

Your Country Requires Your Services

The Indians have assumed a hostile attitude and have invaded the state in violation of the treaty of last summer. The British band of Sacs and other hostile Indians, headed by Black Hawk, are in possession of the Rock River country, to the great terror of the frontier inhabitants. . . . No citizen ought to remain inactive when his country is invaded and the helpless part of the citizenry are in danger.

When the governor called for volunteers to form a militia, Lincoln volunteered on April 19. Two days later, the men of his company elected him their captain. This was Lincoln's first popular triumph, and it gave him no end of satisfaction.

Mosquito Battles

Lincoln and his men joined a detachment of the regular army in a long march north along the Rock River. Spring cloudbursts turned the land into a muddy quagmire. The men encountered no Indians, no action, no glorious battles—only tedious and uncomfortable walking and camping. Captain Lincoln was reprimanded twice, once for letting some of his men get drunk and once for firing a gun in the camp.

Most of the New Salem men went home when their 30-day enlistments ended. Lincoln stayed on until July, marching with the army into the wilderness of southern Wisconsin in search of Chief Black Hawk. But he never saw the elusive Indian chief, or, for that matter, any Indians at all. He was later to joke that the only blood he lost in his country's service was to the swarms of mosquitoes that rose up at every step of the campaign.

But he did see some traces of the bitter Black Hawk War. Once he came across the bodies of five whites who had been killed and scalped. "The red light of the morning sun was streaming upon them as they lay head toward us on the ground," he said, "and every man had a round, red spot on top of his head."

His three months in the Black Hawk War was the extent of Lincoln's military service, for which the state rewarded him with $125 and a small grant of land in Iowa. He returned to New Salem to take up his political campaign for the state legislature just two weeks before election day.

First Elected Office

Lincoln entered American politics at an exciting time. The country was growing rapidly as new states were being added to the Union and settlers were pushing westward. There had been 17 states when Lincoln was born; now, in 1832, there were 24. And as the farmers and backwoodsmen of the Midwest and South increased in number, the nation's political parties began to change.

The first political parties had been based on the East Coast. They were the Federalist Party of George Washington and John Adams and the Jeffersonian Republican Party of Thomas Jefferson and James Monroe. By the middle of the 1820s, the Federalist Party had almost died out, and the Republican Party had split into two rival groups. In the presidential election of 1828, one of these groups favored John Quincy Adams of Massachusetts and Henry Clay of Kentucky for President and Vice-President, respectively; the other group supported Andrew Jackson of Tennessee and John C. Calhoun of South Carolina. When Jackson was elected President, his followers changed their name to the Democratic

Party and supported Jackson for re-election in 1832. Clay, whose supporters eventually formed the Whig Party, was running against him.

Lincoln was a Clay man. He agreed with Clay that the economic life of the nation should be strengthened with such internal improvements as roads and canals and with taxes that favored American-made goods over imported ones. In New Salem, though, local issues held everyone's attention. And here, too, Lincoln came out strongly in favor of economic development.

The big question facing New Salem and other river towns was: Which will come first, the steamboat or the newfangled railroad? The people of New Salem were counting on steamboat traffic to usher in the long-awaited economic and population boom for their town. When a small steamboat finally did chug up the Sangamon River, it was greeted with cheering and wild excitement. But if railroads proved to be more efficient at carrying passengers and freight into the western frontier, river towns like New Salem would be doomed.

Lincoln addressed the question in a typically logical, thorough way. He spent hours on a small boat studying the Sangamon's treacherous currents and mapping its sandbanks and water levels. Finally, he announced in a carefully prepared newspaper article that the Sangamon could be developed to handle river traffic. Clearing away the driftwood and straightening some of the river's bends, he reported, would be less costly than building a railroad. If elected, he would urge the state legislature to adopt this plan, which would ensure a bright future for New Salem and other riverside communities.

In the same newspaper article, his first formal political statement, Lincoln also spoke out in favor of public education, saying that everyone should have enough schooling to be able to read the history of the United States and other nations. Only in this way would America's citizens appreciate the value of their freedom.

In the days before the election, Lincoln campaigned vigorously. He made speeches from tree stumps, as he had done for the amusement of his playmates a few years earlier. He joked and chatted with voters in the fields and around the crackerbarrels of the country stores, and he pitched horseshoes with them at barbecues. But when the votes were counted, Lincoln had lost; he finished eighth of 13 candidates. In his own precinct of New Salem, however, where he was known and greatly liked, he won by an overwhelming majority—227 of the 300 votes cast.

Storekeeper Lincoln

With the election over and Offutt out of business, it was time for Lincoln to look around for a new job. He considered blacksmithing but decided against it. He had long been interested in the law, often hanging around the log courthouses of Little Pigeon Creek, Rockport, and New Salem to listen to the lawyers argue their cases. But he knew he needed more education before he could hope to practice as an attorney. What to do in the meantime?

Sometime in the fall of 1832 Lincoln had an opportunity to buy a half-share in a small general store in New Salem. Although his partner-to-be, William Berry, was an alcoholic and a poor businessman, Lincoln took a chance and bought into the store on credit. He was now a frontier merchant, and he hoped that the store would not only make money but give him a share of importance in the community.

Unfortunately, the partnership was plagued with problems. The store was already in debt, and Lincoln and Berry continued to let their customers buy goods on credit, so that soon they had no money on hand to pay their own bills. Lincoln admitted that he spent too much time talking about politics with his customers, and Berry spent too much time visiting the whiskey barrel in the back room.

Before long, the general store of Lincoln and Berry was overwhelmed by debts. As Lincoln said, it "winked out." Once again, he cast about for a way to support himself.

Hard Work and Hard Times

Lincoln's militia service and his good showing in his precinct when he ran for the state legislature had given him the bare beginnings of a political reputation. So, although he was a Clay supporter, in 1833 he managed to be appointed by re-elected President Jackson as postmaster for New Salem. The part-time position paid $55 a year, along with free use of the mail service for his personal letters and the free delivery of one daily newspaper.

Because he needed more income than the postmaster job paid, Lincoln hired himself out from time to time as a farmhand. He was still a skillful ax-wielder, and his neighbors hired him to split fence rails. No doubt he became depressed at times, remembering how he had hoped to leave the mindless drudgery of farm labor behind him.

Soon, however, Lincoln found a second part-time job. The county surveyor was busy marking property lines and laying out roads as new settlers entered the region. He needed an assistant and offered Lincoln the job, although Lincoln knew nothing about surveying. But just as he had not let the lack of a boat keep him from carrying Denton Offutt's goods to New Orleans, Lincoln did not let the lack of experience keep him from taking on the new job. He borrowed several books on surveying and studied them day and night; he also bought the necessary instruments and a horse on credit. Then he set to work laying out roads, town sites, and homesteads. Often he carried the mail in his hat and delivered it on his way to a surveying site.

Lincoln's postmaster and surveying work enabled him to visit all parts of the county. He met and got to know hundreds of people, most of whom were favorably impressed with this tall, intelligent, dependable young man. The work was hard, requiring him to cover many miles in all sorts of weather, but it helped him build a base of popular recognition and support in preparation for his next attempt at politics.

In the meantime, however, Lincoln's financial situation grew worse. Because he could not pay his debts, the sheriff had to take possession of some of his personal property. Lincoln was most distressed because his horse and his surveying instruments were to be sold at an auction. But some of his friends, who knew that he was working as hard as he could to pay his debts, bought his possessions at the auction and gave them back to him.

A worse blow came in January of 1835, when William Berry died. His death left Lincoln solely responsible for their store's debts, which totalled $1,100—a staggering sum to someone who earned less than $100 a year. Lincoln called it "the National Debt." But instead of moving on to a new area and leaving his unpaid debts behind him, as many other bankrupt men did in those days, Lincoln determined to pay back every cent. It took him nearly 15 years to do so, but it earned him a reputation as an honest and honorable man.

Chapter 4

Introduction to Politics

In 1833 and 1834, while Lincoln was struggling with his debts and his jobs, he was also preparing himself for a second try at politics. He ran for the state legislature in 1834.

By this time, party feeling had grown quite strong in Illinois and across the nation. The Democrats supported President Jackson's policies, which favored states' rights—that is, giving the states power to control their own affairs with little interference from the central government. The Whigs, who rallied behind Senator Henry Clay, believed that a strong central, or federal, government was best to make sure that all parts of the country worked together for the national good.

INTO THE FRAY

Lincoln was a Whig and a firm believer in national unity and a strong federal government. But his campaign for the state legislature was not really based on party issues. He gave few formal speeches and did not offer a written statement as he had done in 1832. Instead, he visited informally with the county voters, listening to their concerns and simply passing the time of day with them. He even competed with 30 farm-hands working in a wheat field to see who could do the most work in a certain amount of time. He won the contest—and their 30 votes.

On election day, members of both parties, as well as some people who hadn't made up their minds about which party to support, voted for Lincoln. He placed second of 13 candidates and was one of four Whigs from Sangamon County who were elected to two-year terms in the Illinois House of Representatives.

Vandalia

The legislature was scheduled to meet in December in Vandalia, the state capital. Lincoln borrowed $200 from a friend, with which he paid his most urgent bills and bought a $60 suit, the first one he had ever owned. At dawn one morning, he threw a single bag on top of a four-horse stagecoach and climbed inside for the ride to Springfield and then south to Vandalia. His political life was about to begin.

Vandalia was a small, dirty town of about 800 people. Its only real business was the state government. Lincoln roomed in a tavern with some other Whig congressmen and quickly got to know his fellow legislators. His best friend among them was John Todd Stuart, whom he had met during the campaign.

Like Lincoln, Stuart had been born in Kentucky, but he had had the advantages of a well-to-do home and an education; his father was a preacher and college professor. Stuart now lived in Springfield, where he had a law practice. Lincoln softened his blunt frontier manners by observing Stuart's more polished ones.

Lincoln's first legislative session was uneventful. The freshman lawmaker served on 12 committees and voted in favor of a state bank and a canal. He studied the tactics of lobbyists, speech-makers, and shrewd politicians from both parties. But his biggest contribution was writing several bills for Whig congressmen who lacked his logical and sharp writing skills. During his early years in the legislature, Lincoln made a name for himself as a good writer.

The first legislative session ended in February. Because lawmakers were paid only while the legislature was actually in session, Lincoln needed to find work with which to support himself, and Stuart suggested the law. The idea appealed to Lincoln, who had already been interested in court cases for some years. He had also served on several juries in New Salem and Springfield, and he may even have argued a few cases as an amateur attorney. But, as he had asked himself before, could someone without a formal education hope to enter the legal profession?

Stuart pointed out to Lincoln that many prairie and frontier lawyers had not gone to school. Most of them had studied law informally while working as a clerk or assistant in the office of an established lawyer. He also said that because Lincoln could read and write, all he had to do to become a lawyer was pass the state's bar examination. Lincoln was encouraged; he carried a bag of borrowed law books back to New Salem and began to teach himself the law.

That spring and summer the people of New Salem grew accustomed to the sight of their lanky legislator walking through the fields holding a book in one hand and reading aloud from it while he waved the other hand in the air. Sometimes he lay on his back under a shade tree with his legs stretched up the trunk. He memorized Blackstone's *Commentaries*, a classic work about the law, and studied many other books, often arguing both sides of a case with himself. Because of his strong desire to establish himself in a profession, his keen memory, and his sharp wit, he made rapid progress.

A Legendary Love Affair

That summer brought tragedy into Lincoln's life. Since his arrival in New Salem, he had been friendly with Ann Rutledge, the pretty, auburn-haired daughter of tavern-owner James Rutledge. He often visited Ann's family and clearly enjoyed her company, and there was no doubt that Ann was fond of him as well. In August she became ill and died at age 22.

Ann's death deeply saddened Lincoln and caused him to brood about the futility of human hopes and the injustice of death. He fell into a serious depression. At that time, such spells of prolonged melancholy were usually called hypochondria, or "hypo." The attack of "hypo" that Lincoln experienced after Ann's death was the first of many. Only the demands of work could pull him out of these black moods.

The tragedy of Ann's early death and Lincoln's deep mourning gave rise to the legend that he was in love with her. This story became popular after Lincoln's death, when it was repeated in several books about him. But, although it is a romantic tale, there is no evidence at all that it is true. Most historians today believe that Ann and Lincoln were simply friends.

A Popular Whig

The second session of Lincoln's legislative term met from December 1835 to February 1836. This session featured the first state political convention to nominate a candidate for President. It was held by the Democrats, under the leadership of Stephen A. Douglas, a short, fiercely argumentative lawyer who championed President Jackson's successor, Martin Van Buren.

Lincoln and the other Whigs disapproved of the convention system. They felt that it was more democratic to allow anyone to run for President simply by announcing his candidacy, without the support of a party. But party politics and conventions were the wave of the future, and eventually Lincoln would participate in them.

Lincoln's own campaign for re-election to the state legislature got under way as soon as the 1835–1836 session ended. He spoke at Whig rallies in New Salem, Petersburg, and Springfield, with his friend Jack Armstrong and the other Clary Grove Boys along to keep order in the crowd and lead the cheering. By now, Lincoln had become popular with the general public and had earned the respect of the influential leaders and decision-makers of the community. He was easily re-elected to another two years in the state House of Representatives; he was re-elected again in 1838 and in 1840, giving him four consecutive terms, or a total of eight years, in office.

An Awkward Courtship

During the summer of 1836, while he campaigned and pored over his law books in New Salem, Lincoln received a strange proposal. Three years earlier he had met a Kentucky girl named Mary Owens while she was visiting her married sister, Mrs. Bennett Abell, in New Salem. Now Mrs. Abell told Lincoln that she was about to visit her family in Kentucky. She would bring Mary back with her, Mrs. Abell said, if Lincoln was interested in marrying her.

Lincoln was surprised and treated the matter as something of a joke. He said that he thought Mary was agreeable and "saw no objection to plodding through life hand in hand with her." The joke was on Lincoln, however, when Mrs. Abell returned from Kentucky shortly thereafter with Mary in tow.

The girl whom Lincoln remembered as pretty and flirtatious had gained some weight, lost some teeth, and become stiff and dull in manner. Here was a dilemma—was he to regard himself as engaged to this woman or not? Lincoln and Mary spent some time together and exchanged notes and letters during the fall, and Mary seemed no more pleased with Lincoln than he was with her. She complained that he had a moody disposition and ungallant backwoods manners. Although the New Salem gossips hinted at an engagement, Lincoln and Mary agreed only that they would write to one another when he returned to the legislature in December of 1836. But alone in Vandalia that winter, troubled with an illness that dragged his spirits down, Lincoln discovered that he missed Mary and was unhappy when he didn't receive letters from her. He wrote to her often.

In March of 1837, after the legislature disbanded, Lincoln took and passed his bar exams. He was now a qualified lawyer, ready to start a new professional career, and he decided to move. Springfield had just replaced Vandalia as the state capital, and it made sense for Lincoln to settle there. He would be close to the legislature, to his friend John Todd Stuart, and to other friends he had made in the legislature. In addition, Springfield was a fast-growing city where he would be sure to find plenty of work to support a new law practice.

Lincoln made a farewell visit to New Salem in April to pack his possessions and say goodbye to friends. Mary had returned to her family in Kentucky, and Lincoln was more confused about their relationship than ever. She visited Springfield in August, but the two remained dissatisfied with one another. Still, they did not manage to clarify the nature of their relationship, and Lincoln felt himself bound by his "promise" to Mrs. Abell to marry Mary—if she wanted to marry him.

Springfield, Illinois, the new state capital, was Lincoln's home from 1837 until his death. One of his law offices was located on this street. (Library of Congress.)

After she left Springfield for Kentucky, Lincoln wrote Mary a long, awkward letter. In it, he left the question of their marriage entirely up to her. If she did not wish to marry him, he said, he released her from any obligation she might feel toward him, yet he hoped that their friendly "acquaintance" would continue. If she did wish to get married, however, he told her, nothing would make him happier. He concluded by saying that, if she preferred not to answer him, he wished her "farewell — a long life and a merry one attend you."

Mary Owens never replied to this letter. Perhaps she was put off by its generally unromantic tone and sensed Lincoln's lack of enthusiasm; perhaps she had simply lost all interest in her almost suitor. For his part, Lincoln revealed a vein of maliciousness when he later mocked her to some friends. He made fun of her claim to be only a month or two older than he. "Nothing," he wrote, "could have commenced at the size of infancy, and reached her present bulk in less than 35 or 40 years."

Springfield Law and Politics

New Salem did not long outlive Lincoln's departure. The Sangamon River, it turned out, had proved impractical for steamboat traffic, and the railroads were stretching farther across the plains every month. The economic boom that was to have arrived by river never came, and people started drifting away to more prosperous communities in the late 1830s. By 1840, the town was all but dead. It is remembered today only because it was home to Abraham Lincoln for six years while he made his start in politics.

The 28-year-old Lincoln had just seven dollars to his name when he arrived in Springfield, where he went into partnership with Stuart. The two men shared a small, dark office in an upstairs room in the circuit-court building. At first, Lincoln slept on a bed in the office, but he soon found a new home. Joshua Speed, a friend who owned a general store, invited him to share his own living quarters above the store. It is said that Speed burst into laughter on moving day, when Lincoln picked up his saddlebags, climbed the stairs, dumped the bags on the floor, and said, "Well, Speed, I'm moved."

Speed soon became a close comrade. Lincoln, Speed, and other young bachelors would gather around the fireplace in the store and swap stories and jokes. Sometimes they talked politics, too, and sometimes Stephen A. Douglas, the fiery Democrat, was a member of the group. He and Lincoln would have many memorable arguments in Speed's store and elsewhere in the years to come.

Lincoln continued to read poetry and to increase his knowledge of the law by studying casebooks and journals. His favorite reading, however, was the newspapers. He read every one he could get his hands on and hated to miss an issue. He kept himself as fully informed of national events and trends as possible.

During the sessions of the state legislature, Lincoln worked tirelessly for bills and projects he believed in, whether they were sponsored by Whigs or Democrats—although most of them were, in fact, Whig measures. One of his greatest interests was a plan to improve transportation throughout the state by means of new and improved roads, canals, railroads, and bridges. This plan fit in well with the overall goals of the national Whig party, which encouraged commerce and cooperation among the different states and regions of the country.

Around the time of his move to Springfield, Lincoln became increasingly aware of a conflict brewing between the South and the North. It was an issue that would someday threaten the life of the nation, dominate his presidency, and wrench his soul. The issue was slavery.

ABOLITIONISTS VERSUS SLAVE OWNERS

Slavery began in the New World in the early 1500s, when the Spanish and Portuguese brought black slaves from Africa to their colonies in the Americas. It started in North America in 1619, when the first black slaves were sold to tobacco planters in the British colony of Virginia. By 1790, soon after the American Revolution and the adoption of the Constitution, there were about 200,000 black slaves in Virginia, and slavery had become entrenched as a way of life for southern tobacco and cotton growers. By Lincoln's time, there were several million slaves in the South.

Slavery rested on a way of thinking and a social structure that allowed some people to regard other people purely as objects — as property no different from cattle or dogs. Slavery is a very old institution; the Egyptians, Greeks, Romans, and other ancient peoples had kept slaves, often prisoners of war or captured populations. But American slavery was different, because it was based on one characteristic only: race. It may be difficult for us today to understand how one race could believe it was permissible to enslave another, but it was possible for many southern whites to believe this because they thought that their black slaves were not really people. Blacks were regarded as a completely separate species, and there was very little contact between most blacks and most whites, even on plantations in the Deep South.

Because they had little or no chance to learn otherwise, many whites truly believed that black people were meant to be slaves, were incapable of learning or self-government, and had no culture. This made it possible for some southern whites to justify slave-holding and to feel no guilt about it. Other southerners — perhaps less certain of the inferiority of black people — were deeply fearful of blacks and felt that they had to be "kept in their place" or they might challenge white supremacy.

On top of what was perceived to be a profound and unbridgeable gulf between the races, slavery was essentially an economic institution. The South began as a region of large farms and few businesses or industries; as such, it needed cheap labor. The North, on the other hand, was from the start a region of small family farms and businesses; this helped keep slavery from gaining a foothold in the North.

Another factor that kept slavery out of the North was religion. A religious and humanitarian movement against the slave trade had arisen in England as early as the mid-1700s. Its leaders were mostly Quakers, and their influence was strong in the northern colonies. Few slaves were ever brought to the North. When European countries started outlawing slavery in the late 1700s and early 1800s, the northern states followed suit. Vermont was the first to ban slavery, in 1777; New Jersey was the last, in 1804. Most of the slaves who were freed in the North did not remain there but were sent to the South.

The Founding Fathers and Slavery

Lincoln knew from his reading that the country's founding fathers, men like George Washington and Thomas Jefferson, had been deeply troubled by the existence of slavery in a nation whose Declaration of Independence contained the words "All Men are created equal." Jefferson, in fact, acknowledged that slavery was immoral when he wrote, "I tremble for my country when I reflect that God is just." But while many of the country's early leaders had believed slavery was wrong, they did not know how to end it, for they believed that free black people could not live together with whites in the same society. In addition, some people believed it would be unfair to threaten the livelihoods of southerners by taking away the slaves.

So the founding fathers compromised. In 1787, slavery was forbidden in the Northwest Territory, the new lands beyond the Ohio River. But that same year, the framers of the Constitution agreed not to mention slavery, because South Carolina and Georgia threatened not to join the Union if their slaveholding rights were menaced.

Jefferson and James Monroe, among others, hoped that slavery would gradually die out as more and more people became convinced that it was wrong. They also felt that, as blacks and whites could not be expected to live together, the freed black people should be established in new homes overseas — in Africa, perhaps, or the Caribbean. This policy, which was called colonization, was tried several times; the

modern African nation of Liberia, in fact, began as a colony
for freed American slaves. But the colonization of huge num-
bers of former slaves was clearly impractical, and, besides,
many of them did not want to leave the United States.
So the dilemma remained and grew. Some people,
mostly in the South, believed that blacks were inferior be-
ings and that slavery was part of the natural order of things.
Others, mostly in the North, believed that slavery was immoral and should be ended at once. The latter group came
to be called abolitionists, because they wanted to abolish
slavery—that is, to end it completely and immediately. In between the two groups were many people, like Lincoln, who
recognized and were troubled by the complexity of the issue.

Lincoln believed that slavery was morally wrong, that
no man had the right to own another. But he did not see eye
to eye with the abolitionists, for he felt that the immediate
end of slavery would bring about a devastating social and economic crisis in the South. Further, what was to be done with
the freed slaves if the abolitionists had their way? Like many
others who hated slavery, Lincoln was for a long time unable to imagine blacks and whites living together as equals
in an integrated nation. He hoped that slavery would diminish over time and that, eventually, some way could be found
to remove the blacks from the United States. As far as immediate action was concerned, Lincoln was firmly opposed
to the extension of slavery outside the original slave states
of the South. The evil was already bad enough, he felt; it
must be contained, not allowed to spread further.

Cotton and Compromise

Any hope that slavery would diminish over time was most
likely shattered in 1793, when Eli Whitney invented the cotton gin. This machine separated cotton seeds from the plant's

fibers, a task that was formerly done by hand. A slave working by the old method could produce about one pound of pure
cotton a day; the yield of the cotton gin was 50 pounds per
day—and the British textile industry was eager to buy as much
American cotton as it could.

When the southern plantation owners suddenly found
themselves able to process more cotton, they decided to grow
more cotton. Naturally, they then needed more slaves. The
number of American slaves increased greatly during the early
years of the 19th century. In order to protect their interests
in the national Congress, the southern states insisted that one
new slave state shall be admitted to the Union for each new
free state—this meant that the senators of the slave states could
not be outvoted by those from the free states. In 1820, President James Monroe negotiated the Missouri Compromise,
which divided the newly acquired Louisiana Territory into
a slave zone and a free zone.

During the 1830s, the South became more and more determined to uphold, justify, and extend the slave system. But
opposition to slavery gained strength, too. The voices of the
abolitionists began to be heard throughout the land. A clash
between slave owners and abolitionists seemed imminent. Fur-
thermore, a series of slave uprisings, dating from about 1800,
had filled southern whites with fear of blacks. The revolts
were mercilessly quelled, but southerners now worried that
the abolitionists might encourage more revolts.

Lincoln's state, Illinois, had outlawed slavery. Yet many
citizens and legislators in Illinois were sympathetic to the
southern cause. Above all, they feared that if slavery were
abolished, a horde of freed blacks would enter Illinois. They
would compete for jobs, sit on juries, go to public schools,
and run for office; they might even wish to marry whites.

So most people in Illinois disliked the abolitionists, who
were characterized as Eastern busybodies. The people of some

Tension and hostility between slave owners and abolitionists rose to fever pitch during the years after Lincoln entered politics. That hostility eventually erupted into violence, as in this scene of a massacre of five proslavery men by abolitionist John Brown and his followers. (Library of Congress.)

southern states went even further. Communities in North Carolina, Georgia, Alabama, and Louisiana openly offered cash bounties for prominent northern abolitionists, dead or alive. And politicians in Missouri vowed to kill any abolitionist who entered their state.

A Riot in Alton

In November of 1837, during Lincoln's second term in the state legislature, a mob murdered Elijah Lovejoy, the editor of an abolitionist newspaper in Alton, Illinois, burned his office, and threw his printing press into the Mississippi River. This tragic event alarmed many people across the nation. Former President John Quincy Adams said that the incident was "a shock as of any earthquake throughout this continent."

Soon after the Alton incident, some Illinois legislators introduced a resolution that condemned antislavery societies and newspapers because they provoked violence. Not only did Lincoln refuse to vote for these resolutions, but he and another member of the House of Representatives wrote a protest against them. It condemned slavery as both immoral and dangerous, as "injustice and bad policy."

A few weeks later, in January of 1838, Lincoln made a speech at a young men's club in Springfield. His subject was violence in America. Mob violence, he warned, threatened not just the abolitionists but the very rights on which the nation was founded: freedom of speech, protection under the law, government by elected representatives. He urged his listeners to "swear by the blood of the Revolution" to respect the law and to act out of reason, not out of angry passion. If they did not do so, he declared, "depend upon it, the Government cannot last."

Chapter 5

The Lawyer in Love

L incoln's writing and speech-making skills won him growing recognition and importance in the Whig Party and in the state of Illinois. He was the Whig speaker on the floor of the House of Representatives from 1836 on. He also served as chairman of the legislature's Finance Committee. He was appointed to the Whig Central Committee, which selected candidates for statewide office. And, as a prominent member of the Young Whigs Organization, he took part in frequent debates with Stephen A. Douglas and other Young Democrats.

The Democratic Party gained strength across the nation as the 1840 elections approached. Fearful that Democratic presidential candidate Martin Van Buren would be elected for a second term, the Whigs campaigned vigorously for their candidate, William Henry Harrison. In Illinois, Lincoln was very active during the spring and summer, campaigning both on behalf of Harrison and for re-election to his own seat in the state legislature.

THE 1840 ELECTION

The Whig campaign portrayed Van Buren, the Democrat, as a snobbish Eastern aristocrat who dined on elegant meals and drank fancy foreign wines — someone, in short, who would be unsympathetic to the needs of the common people of the Midwest and West. Harrison, on the other hand, was said to be a simple man of the people, an ordinary fellow who would be satisfied with a log cabin and a jug of cider. Thus, the 1840 presidential campaign came to be called the log-cabin-and-cider campaign. Whigs passed out badges in the shape of log cabins, sang backwoods songs at rallies, and formed Log Cabin Clubs.

Lincoln made speeches at many of these rallies and clubs. But he did not emphasize his own rustic background, so similar to the Whig portrait of Harrison, because he was not particularly proud of that part of his life. He wanted to be recognized as a hard-working, thoughtful, professional man, not as a backwoods bumpkin who had made good. Nevertheless, his close involvement in the log-cabin campaign of 1840 contributed to his own later image as the rail-splitting prairie President.

After a hard-fought campaign, which included a number of lively debates with Douglas, the election was a disappointment to Lincoln. Although Harrison won the presidency, Van Buren carried Illinois and the Democrats won control of the state legislature. Lincoln himself was re-elected – but just barely. He placed last of five Whigs who were sent to Springfield. It was his worst showing since the election he had lost in 1832.

A PROSPEROUS PRACTICE

In the meantime, however, Lincoln had become a thriving lawyer, as he and Stuart built a successful practice. In 1840 Lincoln defended his first case before the Illinois Supreme Court. But Stuart had been elected to the United States House of Representatives in 1838, and thereafter he spent a great deal of time in Washington, D.C.

Because both Stuart and Lincoln had become wrapped up in politics, each man soon realized that he needed a partner who could be more involved in the day-to-day details of maintaining a law practice: keeping the books, writing letters to clients, and other chores that both Stuart and Lincoln hated. So, in the spring of 1841, they dissolved their partnership, although they remained friends.

A New Partner

Lincoln then formed a new partnership with Stephen T. Logan. Like Lincoln and Stuart, Logan was a Whig, but he was not so deeply involved in politics. He was a short, wrinkled, red-haired man who dressed in baggy pants and a battered straw hat. And he was a man of peculiar habits. For one thing, he was addicted to whittling, even in court. At the beginning of each day, a courtroom attendant would hand him a pile of wooden shingles and a sack for his shavings.

Despite his eccentricity, Logan was a respected and successful lawyer, with a precise, meticulous attention to practical details that was the perfect match for Lincoln's own broader interests in theory and philosophy. The law firm of Logan and Lincoln soon became one of the busiest in the Springfield area.

Within a few years of his arrival in Springfield, Lincoln was earning between $1,200 and $1,500 a year—at a time when the governor of the state received a salary of $1,200 and circuit-court judges received $750. He invested some of his income in real estate; he also continued to make payments on his old New Salem debts. At last, he was on the rise in his chosen profession. But at the same time, he was suffering setbacks in other areas of his life.

For one thing, the state Whig organization did not nominate Lincoln to run in 1841 for a fifth term in the state legislature. He wasn't sure whether he minded it or not. On the one hand, he loved the excitement of politics and had hoped to remain a part of it. On the other hand, he had learned a lot in eight years and had become tired of state politics. He wondered if he was ready to try his wings in a larger political arena. Maybe be could get elected to the national Congress, like his friend Stuart. In a year or so, he would see. But in the meantime, his thoughts and feelings were deeply engaged in another matter.

LINCOLN IN LOVE

In December 1839 Lincoln attended a gala party in Springfield. Everyone was there: Douglas, Lincoln's friends Speed and Stuart, and a fashionable young couple named Ninian and Elizabeth Edwards (Elizabeth was a cousin of Stuart). During the course of the party, Lincoln met Mrs. Edwards' sister, who was visiting from Lexington, Kentucky. Her name was Mary Ann Todd.

Lincoln was usually somewhat shy at social events, especially around women. He was painfully conscious of his gawky homeliness and his lack of a stylish upbringing. He did not expect the popular young women to like him. But Mary Todd was different.

True, Mary Ann Todd was exceptionally popular. Although she was a trifle plump, her sparkling dark eyes, winsome smile, and vivacious manner made her very attractive. She was 21 years old, nine years younger than Lincoln. She dressed elegantly and danced the latest steps to perfection. And her background couldn't have been further removed from Lincoln's. Her father was a wealthy banker, and she had been pampered, waited on by slaves, and treated with every luxury. Nevertheless, she was gracious, intelligent, interested in politics and the world around her—and she seemed interested in Lincoln, too. He wanted to see her again.

Before long, Lincoln was a regular caller at the Edwardses' hilltop home. He and Mary would sit side by side on a shiny horsehair sofa; Mary would chatter while Lincoln balanced a teacup on his knee and listened and looked. He liked her bright manner, and he rejoiced that she understood and cared about politics and government, the subjects so dear to his heart. Indeed, Mary's father was a prominent Kentucky Whig and a friend of Lincoln's idol, Henry Clay. They talked about Clay, about the law, about poems and plays. Before long, Lincoln found himself—for the first time in his life—deeply in love.

Mary returned his feelings. Beneath his shyness she sensed energy, intelligence, and ambition. She admired him for having overcome the limitations of his background to achieve success, and she respected his wit and intelligence. He was, she said, "the most congenial mind" she had ever met. She had had other suitors; she even flirted briefly with Stephen A. Douglas, Lincoln's Democratic rival. But she was drawn to Lincoln as never before to another man.

A Troubled Romance

Lincoln and Mary continued to see each other throughout 1840, and the courtship grew serious. At some point, they began to talk about marriage. To friends, Lincoln confessed that he sometimes doubted whether, with his humble background and his lack of sophistication, he could ever make a refined creature like Mary happy. But for her part, "Molly," as he called her, declared that she cared about him, not about his background. By December, a year after their first meeting, Lincoln and Mary apparently announced an "understanding," an informal engagement.

The news was not well received by Mary's family. Elizabeth and Ninian Edwards liked Lincoln well enough as an acquaintance, but they did not think he was good enough to marry Mary. He had no respectable family connections, and his income, while good by average standards, did not equal those of the Edwardses and Todds. Elizabeth Edwards in particular became quite hostile to Lincoln. She informed him that he was no longer welcome in her home.

From Lexington, too, came a series of agitated letters from Mary's father, vehemently opposing the proposed match to a young nobody. Mary cried and complained bitterly about the unfairness of it all, but Lincoln was more deeply wounded. He was dismayed that, after working so desperately hard to educate himself, to attain a reputation for honesty and diligence, to win an elected office and own a thriving business, he still suffered from the obscurity and poverty of his origins.

Lincoln had kept himself distant from his family since moving to New Salem on his own in 1831. He never visited and seldom sent letters or messages. He did not want his lack of family respectability to hurt his career, and he wanted even less to be reminded of the backwoods life he had left behind. Yet now it appeared that he hadn't really left it behind after all. Depressed with an attack of the "hypo," Lincoln said resentfully to a friend that one "d" was enough for God, but the Todds had to have two.

"The Fatal First"

Afterward, Lincoln was to refer to New Year's Day, 1841, as "the fatal first of January." On that day, Lincoln wrote Mary to ask her to release him from their understanding. Her family's opposition had destroyed his confidence in himself, and he feared now that he could never support her or make her happy. Although his letter hurt and saddened Mary, she understood what Lincoln was feeling and gracefully agreed to the end of the understanding.

The following few months were a period of dark despair for Lincoln. He underwent one of the worst spells of depression of his life. He remained in bed for one whole week in January, unable to work, sleep, or eat. "If what I feel were equally distributed to the whole human family," he wrote to Stuart, "there would not be one cheerful face on earth." He believed he had lost Mary for good, and he doubted his self-worth after the way he had been treated by the Edwardses.

Everything else seemed to be falling apart, too. His legislative term ended in March, with no renomination. His partnership with Stuart ended in May. Joshua Speed sold his store, and Lincoln had to take a new room alone. To make matters worse, Speed was moving back to Kentucky.

Speed had been Lincoln's closest friend for more than three years. Only to him did Lincoln reveal the full depth of his unhappiness over Mary. More than anyone else at that time, Speed understood his friend's complex personality. He knew both sides of Lincoln: the cheerful and humorous side that loved to crack jokes with friends and worked like a demon, and the other side that was tormented by doubts and moodiness, the side that caused Speed to say, "I never saw so gloomy and melancholy a face in all my life."

By summer, the town gossips were whispering about Mary's new admirer, a middle-aged widower with two children. Mary, however, did not take him seriously, for she was still in love with Lincoln. As for Lincoln, he continued to be truly unhappy about his failure with Mary, but at least he had snapped out of his "hypo." His new partnership with Logan was off to a good start, and he had plenty of work to keep him busy. In August, he visited Speed, who was living with his family in Kentucky. Like Lincoln, Speed was also in the middle of an unhappy love affair, and the two men sympathized with each other's troubles.

Speed decided to accompany Lincoln back to Springfield for a visit. An incident during the trip made a deep and lasting impression on Lincoln. On a steamboat on the Ohio River, they saw 12 black slaves who were being sold away from their homes and families in Kentucky to new masters in the Deep South. The 12 were chained together, as Lincoln said, "like fish on a line." The sight disturbed and haunted him. Years later he reminded Speed of the incident, saying that the memory of those 12 slaves "was a continual torment."

Obstacles Overcome

Back in Springfield, Lincoln avoided Mary but could not stop thinking about her. He worked hard and began to regain his self-confidence and optimism. Lincoln was delighted when Speed wrote from Kentucky in early 1842 that he had married his sweetheart. He began to wonder if there was any hope for him with Mary after all, especially because he had heard from mutual friends that she still cared for him.

Finally, a local hostess arranged a meeting between the two lovers, who had been separated for nearly a year and a half. They discovered that their affection for one another was as strong as ever. Lincoln began courting Mary all over again—but this time he met her at friends' homes, not at the Edwards mansion.

In the fall of 1842, while Lincoln and Mary were rebuilding their romance, Lincoln took part in an incident that caused him great embarrassment. He wrote at least one of a series of anonymous newspaper articles that poked savage fun at James Shields, a pompous Democrat who was the state auditor. Evidence shows that Mary and a girlfriend also wrote one or more of the articles, which were filled with funny but crude personal insults. Shields was outraged and demanded to know the author's name. When Lincoln admitted authorship, gallantly leaving the young women out of it, Shields promptly challenged Lincoln to a duel!

Springfield seethed with rumors about the matter. Lincoln wrote to Shields, explaining that the articles were intended as a political statement, not a personal attack, but Shields was not satisfied with this explanation—which, in truth, was a little lame. Finally, Lincoln accepted Shields' challenge, but only on the condition that the two men fight it out with cavalry broadswords inside an eight-foot circle. Obviously, Lincoln was trying to turn the whole affair into a joke, but Shields grimly agreed to Lincoln's ludicrous condition. The two men met on September 22 across the state border in Missouri. Fortunately, they were accompanied by friends who managed to calm them down and talk them out of their rash plan.

Afterward, Lincoln was ashamed of his part in the affair and never referred to it again. But he never again turned his considerable wit against another person in the form of cruel satire, for he had seen its painful consequences firsthand. For the rest of his life, Lincoln detested the thought of personal violence and responded to insults or threats by laughing or walking away.

Mary was grateful to Lincoln for keeping her name out of the Shields scandal. After spending much time together in October, Lincoln proposed to her again. She accepted, and they set November 4 as their wedding day.

Lincoln and Mary did not tell Ninian and Elizabeth Edwards of their plan until the very morning of the wedding. The Edwardses received the news with dismay, but when they saw how determined Mary was, they gave in and offered to have the wedding in their home. That evening, Lincoln and

Mary were married by an Episcopal minister in the Edwards' parlor, with a few friends on hand. Lincoln gave his bride a ring engraved with the words "Love Is Eternal."

Lincoln's family was not present. Thomas Lincoln learned of his son's marriage months later, when Lincoln was in Coles County on business and stopped to visit his parents.

Married Life

The Lincolns settled into their first home on the night they were married. It was a single room above the Globe Tavern that Lincoln rented for $4 a week. This was the best he could afford, because he was still paying his New Salem debts. And now he was trying to save money for a home and family.

Life at the Globe was hard for Mary, who had been surrounded by slaves at her family's home and waited on by servants at the Edwards' home. It bothered her that their wealthier friends sometimes belittled the Lincolns' humble quarters, but she did her best to get along. She also missed having a lot of money to spend on fashionable clothes, for which she had an almost uncontrollable passion.

Lincoln and Mary's first child, a son, was born on August 1, 1843, at the tavern. They named him Robert Todd after Mary's father. Soon afterward, the Lincolns moved out of the Globe and into a small rented cottage. Then, in January of 1844, with financial help from the Todd family, Lincoln bought a house and lot at the corner of Eighth and Jackson streets for $1,200. The two-story wooden frame house, with tall windows on all sides, a chimney at either end, and a few tall shade trees, was the only home Lincoln ever owned. Today, it is maintained by the government as a national historic site.

The Lincolns were happy in their new home, where their second child, Edward Baker Lincoln, was born in 1846. Be-

This photograph of Lincoln, the earliest one known to exist, was probably made in Springfield in 1846, around the time Edward Baker Lincoln was born. Lincoln was a happy husband and father, as well as a busy lawyer. His involvement in national politics was about to begin. (Library of Congress.)

fore long, Lincoln was able to hire a maid for Mary, so that she could spend more time shopping and visiting with her friends.

Mary and Lincoln got along well together during these years. She was proud of his successes in the courtroom and was delighted that he was a loving, affectionate father. She defended him fiercely to anyone who criticized his appearance, politics, or manners. Yet she was troubled by insecurities, too.

The year at the Globe Tavern had given Mary a horror of poverty. She loved to buy fine furnishings for her home and especially to buy clothing and jewelry. But after she came home from her shopping trips, she worried that her heavy spending would ruin the family financially. She grew anxious about her appearance and desperately eager for compliments and attention. Lincoln humored these needs, soothing her raging headaches and making her smile by calling her his "child wife."

Occasionally, Mary and Lincoln had difficulties, as all married couples do. These were usually brought about by Mary's impatience with Lincoln's moodiness or fits of the "hypo." Although Mary sometimes became shrill and hysterical, Lincoln never argued with her; he simply avoided her until she had calmed down. Most of the time, however, they were tender and attentive to one another. All in all, their marriage was a loving and happy one.

A NEW LAW PRACTICE

In December of 1844, Lincoln and Stephen Logan dissolved their law partnership. Lincoln had first been Stuart's junior partner and then Logan's. Now, at age 35, he was ready to set up a law office of his own, with his own junior partner.

He selected William Herndon, whom he called Billy. Nine years younger than Lincoln, Herndon talked and drank a lot, but he was intelligent and willing to work hard. And he admired Lincoln very much.

Lincoln and Herndon settled into a dusty second-floor office on Springfield's main square. At first, Herndon carried books, looked up articles, and ran errands for Lincoln. Soon, though, he was handling cases of his own with great skill. And before long, the firm was extremely busy, with about 100 cases a year.

Neither Lincoln nor Herndon was particularly neat or well organized, and their office had a decidedly scruffy look. Piles of papers lay everywhere. They never swept the floor, so drifts of dust and dirt formed under the rickety cane chairs, the desks, and the sofa where Lincoln liked to sprawl as he wrote. Visitors joked that the orange seeds that dropped from Lincoln's lunches were likely to sprout in the topsoil that had accumulated on the floor.

As they worked closely together for many hours a day over a period of years, Lincoln and Herndon became good friends. Herndon worshipped Lincoln's ambition, wisdom, and high ideals. In turn, Lincoln appreciated Herndon's loyalty and his dedication to work. He came to regard the younger man almost as a son and overlooked his occasional grumpiness and his alcoholism.

Although the two men enjoyed a warm friendship as well as a partnership, Herndon was not very fond of Lincoln's family. He hated it when the indulgent Lincoln would bring his sons to the office on Sundays and calmly do his work while the youngsters overturned inkstands, threw papers about, and generally raised the roof. But although Herndon sometimes wanted to "wring their little necks," he held his temper out of affection for the boys' father.

Herndon didn't get on well with Mary, either. He thought

she was spiteful and cold. She, in turn, thought he was a drunkard and a rogue, and she was not pleased when Lincoln began splitting equally the firm's profits with him. Years later, when Herndon wrote about his friendship with Lincoln, he said a number of harsh things about Mary. His unflattering portrait of her remained fixed in the public mind for generations, although it was far from accurate.

Prairie Law

Lincoln's law practice was part of the Illinois Eighth Circuit, which was a district of 14 counties in central Illinois. The circuit judges traveled from court to court around the district twice a year, for three months at a time. Lincoln and other lawyers who had cases to be heard in the circuit courts followed on horseback.

By now, Springfield had become quite civilized. Elsewhere in the district, however, the roving lawyers faced washed-out roads, flea-infested hotels, and other travelers' hazards. It was grueling work that kept Lincoln away from his home and family for half of each year, but—like his postmaster and surveying jobs back in New Salem—it gave him the chance to meet people from all over the region. He had not given up on politics, and he knew that the contacts he was making and the good reputation he was building in his legal work would be very helpful the next time he ran for public office.

Chapter 6

Congressman Lincoln

Although his family and his law practice kept Lincoln busy during the mid-1840s, he had not lost his interest in politics. In 1844 he campaigned throughout Illinois and Indiana for Henry Clay for President. Clay lost, but Lincoln took advantage of the trip to Indiana to visit his boyhood home at Little Pigeon Creek.

The sight of the homestead and community he had left nearly 15 years before touched Lincoln more deeply than he had expected; in particular, he was saddened to learn that many of the people he remembered had died. As he walked the hills and fields, he started to feel that, as he put it, "every spot was a grave."

For more than a year after Lincoln returned to Little Pigeon Creek, he was subject to spells of melancholic reminiscence. During one of these periods, he tried to express in a poem the mood of sorrowful nostalgia the visit had stirred in him. One verse dealt with a young man who had gone insane during Lincoln's boyhood and had remained mad all the years in between:

> O death! Thou awe-inspiring prince,

That keepst the world in fear;
Why dost thou tear more blest ones hence,
And leave him ling'ring here?

This type of gloomy poetry, full of funeral dirges, distant voices, and gravestones, was quite popular in Lincoln's day — so much so that the editor of a paper called the *Quincy Whig* published Lincoln's 23-verse poem under the title "Return."

Fortunately for both literature and history, Lincoln's verse-making mood soon left him and he turned his attention once more to politics. He hungered for a role in the national government. He had tried in 1843 to get the Whig nomination for candidacy to the United States House of Representatives, but someone else was chosen. In 1845, he decided to try again.

Lincoln spent the summer of 1845 on horseback, touring his congressional district and winning the good will and backing of local Whig party leaders. His lobbying paid off. When the party met in 1846, he was nominated as the district's congressional candidate.

Lincoln's Democratic opponent in the election campaign was a Methodist preacher who accused Lincoln of being an atheist — that is, of denying the existence of God. To support his accusation, he pointed out that Lincoln had never joined a church. In response, Lincoln printed and circulated a handbill about his religious views; it was the only time he ever discussed them publicly. In the handbill, Lincoln assured the voters that, while he was not a church member, he believed in God and the Bible and felt no disrespect for religion. On another occasion he remarked to a friend, "When any church will inscribe over its altar the Saviour's condensed statement of law and gospel: 'Thou shalt love the Lord thy God with all thy soul and with all thy mind, and love thy neighbor as thyself,' that church will I join with all my heart."

THE UNCOMPROMISING CONGRESSMAN

When the votes were counted in August of 1846, Lincoln won by a large majority. But he had to wait more than year before taking his seat in the next session of Congress, which did not meet until December of 1847.

Lincoln and Mary, along with Robert and little Eddie, arrived in Washington, D.C., in early December and took rooms in a boardinghouse that was home to a number of Whigs and abolitionists. By day, Lincoln worked in the Capitol building across the way; in the evenings, he sometimes sat spinning stories with his fellow boarders.

Mary, however, found Washington not much to her liking. It was a muddy, graceless, undeveloped place. Much of the city's spacious beauty was still on the drawing boards, while pigs rooted in the rutted streets, outhouses dotted the vacant lots, and manacled slaves waited morosely outside slave markets to be sold.

Mary was quickly bored with these dismal surroundings, and she grew fretful that Lincoln paid so much attention to his work and his new cronies. After three months, she took the boys with her on a long visit to her father's home in Kentucky. Busy though he was, Lincoln missed his family. He wrote frequently to Mary and enclosed small letters for his sons. "Don't let the blessed fellows forget father," he told her.

Slavery and War

During his term in Congress, Lincoln turned his attention to the issue that had been troubling American society and politics for decades: slavery. He hated the sight of slaves in the nation's capital, and he decided that something should be done about it.

Lincoln came up with a plan to free the slaves in the District of Columbia. It was to be done gradually, with the consent of the slave owners, who would be paid by the government for the value of the slaves they gave up. The plan was not accepted, however, because the abolitionists thought it was too mild, and the slave owners thought it was too harsh. But the problem of slavery continued to nag at Lincoln. He began to foresee that here was an issue that could tear the country apart.

But the big issue during Lincoln's two-year congressional term was the Mexican-American War, or "Mr. Polk's war," as the Whigs liked to call it. The war had broken out in 1846; by the time Lincoln arrived in Congress, U.S. troops were in control of Mexico City. President Polk claimed that Mexico had started the war, but many Whigs believed that Polk and the Democrats had started the war as an excuse for grabbing territory. (At that time, Mexico included much of what is now the southwestern United States.) Lincoln and other Whigs voted to condemn Polk and the war as unjust and misguided. (Of course, one reason the Whigs wanted President Polk to look bad was because they were grooming their own presidential candidate, Zachary Taylor—who, ironically, was a hero of the Mexican-American War.)

In January of 1848, Lincoln did something that almost wrecked his political career. On the floor of Congress, he made a powerful speech that accused Polk of starting a war against peaceful Mexicans. He called Polk "a bewildered, confounded, and miserably perplexed man" whose mind was not equal to the demands of government. And he blamed Polk for not ending the war.

Bad Timing

Although Lincoln's speech was a colorful piece of oratory and a strong statement of Whig opinion, it was also the victim of bad timing. Just two weeks later, Washington received a peace treaty signed by Mexico that turned two-fifths of Mexico's territory over to the United States. The war was over, and the United States had gained California and the whole American Southwest. The nation now stretched from sea to shining sea, and even many of the antiwar Whigs could not help but be pleased about that.

Many people, however, were less than pleased with Lincoln. Back home in Illinois, where Polk and the war had a lot of popular support, the Democratic newspapers raged at Lincoln for his "treasonable assault" on the President and his unpatriotic defense of Mexico. Although a few Whigs still agreed with Lincoln, they felt he had been too outspoken. They did not come to his support because there was nothing to be gained by it: the war was over and the nation in general was quite pleased with its outcome, so criticizing it could only make a politician unpopular. And many people of both parties in Illinois thought that their congressman had disgraced the state and made a fool of himself. Even Billy Herndon wrote Lincoln that he was wrong about the war.

But Lincoln refused to back down. He wrote to Herndon that his opposition to the war was a matter of conscience. He did not believe that the President had the right to make war at will, just to prevent a possible attack or to seize territory. He would stand by his principles.

Lincoln's steadfastness on the war issue seems admirable today, but at the time it appeared likely to end his political career. It made him unpopular in his home state, a laughingstock to the Democrats, and a bit of an embarrassment to the Whigs. Nevertheless, he helped the Whigs elect Taylor President in 1848 by making speeches on Taylor's behalf in Illinois, Maryland, and Massachusetts during the summer.

When Taylor was successful at the polls, Lincoln expected to be rewarded with the post of Commissioner of the General Land Office in Washington. But Taylor appointed someone else to the position, perhaps because of Lincoln's well-publicized opposition to the war in which Taylor had fought with distinction. Later, Taylor offered Lincoln the posts of secretary and then governor of the Oregon Territory, but Lincoln refused. Oregon was too remote and out of the mainstream of political activity. Lincoln did not want to be sent thousands of miles away from his home state and the nation's capital. He still had some hope of salvaging his career in government.

BACK TO THE LAW

For now, however, Lincoln realized that he had to withdraw from politics until the furor aroused by his anti-Polk speech had been forgotten. When his congressional term ended in 1849, he returned to Springfield and the law office of Lincoln and Herndon. He was determined, he wrote later, to practice law "with greater earnestness than ever."

Sadly, Lincoln's homecoming was marred by a personal tragedy. His son Eddie died in February of 1850; he was not quite four years old. Lincoln was grief-stricken, but Mary became almost demented with sorrow. Years later, her son Robert recalled that she remained in her room weeping for weeks. Soon she turned to religion for comfort, just as Lincoln turned to his work.

However, the somber house became cheerful again when a third son, William Wallace, was born in December 1850. Lincoln and Mary called him Willie. Three years later they had a fourth and last child, Thomas; he was called Taddie.

Railroad Attorney

The westward push of the railroads after about 1850 brought new legal work to Lincoln. He handled a number of cases for the railroad companies, helping them obtain legal charters and defending them against taxation. One taxation case he handled for the Illinois Central Railroad brought him the single largest fee of his career, $5,000 — although the company took so long to pay him that he finally had to sue for his money.

In another railroad case, he defended the Rock Island Bridge, the first to cross the Mississippi. When a steamboat hit the railroad bridge and sank, river transportation interests charged that the bridge was dangerous and illegal. Lincoln looked over the bridge, sat down on the edge of the river, and chatted with the bridgemaster and the local people about currents; he even took measurements of the water's speed. He was able to prove in court that the steamboat wreck was the fault of the boat's captain, not of the bridge.

The same attention to detail appeared in another famous lawsuit over a patent for a grain reaper. Lincoln studied the workings of various types of reapers and brought a model machine into the courtroom. His technical explanation of the mechanism's inner workings was so interesting that the jurors left their seats and crouched on the floor beside him to peer at the gears and cogs.

Patent law was of particular interest to Lincoln at this time because he, too, had patented an invention in 1849. It was a contrivance of inflatable rubber-coated cloth balloons that could be used to lighten a vessel and buoy it over shallows and sandbanks in a river. The ingenious device was never put into use, but Lincoln remains the only President to have held a patent.

Murder and Moonshine

Not all of Lincoln's law cases involved big business. As he had done since the start of his legal career, he continued to handle cases for clients large and small: divorces, property disputes, criminal charges. The most famous case of all was probably a murder trial in 1858.

The defendant was a fellow named Duff Armstrong, the son of Lincoln's old friend Jack Armstrong, of the Clary Grove Boys. Young Armstrong and another man had gotten drunk at a revival meeting in August of 1857. That night they allegedly beat a third man so severely that he died a few days later. The star witness against Armstrong testified that he had seen the fight clearly because the full moon was directly overhead. He swore he could not be mistaken about Armstrong's identity.

Lincoln rose to cross-examine the witness. With his thumbs hooked under his suspenders, he confirmed the date and time of the beating. Then he asked the witness, "You say you could not have been mistaken because the full moon was directly overhead and you could see quite clearly?" The witness answered yes—whereupon Lincoln produced an almanac for 1857 and showed the jury that at the hour of the fight, the moon was low in the sky, almost ready to set. If the witness could be utterly wrong about the moon, Lincoln suggested, perhaps he was wrong about Armstrong's identity, too. Armstrong was acquitted.

By the early 1850s, Lincoln was one of the best-known lawyers in Illinois. But although he was busy and quite prosperous, he still had not lost the desire to take part in his country's government. Then, in 1854, he was called out of his political retirement by his old rival, Stephen A. Douglas.

Chapter 7
The Question of Slavery

In Washington and across the nation, the problem of slavery was growing. On one hand, the abolitionists were more fervent than ever in their insistence that the slaves be set free; on the other, the slave owners insisted not only that they would continue to own their slaves but that slavery should be extended into some of the new western territories that were being formed into states. Lincoln agreed with the Whig leader, Senator Henry Clay, who negotiated compromises between the two groups. Although Lincoln personally detested slavery, he could see no good way to end it. At the same time, he did not want to see it spread into new states. He hoped that Clay's tactic of compromise would keep the peace.

THE KANSAS-NEBRASKA ACT

Lincoln's hope for a compromise on the slavery issue was shattered in 1854, when Stephen A. Douglas, now a U.S. senator from Illinois, introduced into Congress the Kansas-Nebraska Act. This act embodied Democrat Douglas' answer to the question of whether slavery should be extended to new territories and states. He called the solution "popular sovereignty," meaning that the people who lived in the territories should decide for themselves whether to allow slavery or not. The passage of the Kansas-Nebraska Act overturned President Monroe's Missouri Compromise of 1820, which had marked off the northern part of the Louisiana Territory as free of slavery forever.

Abolitionists were outraged by the act. So was Lincoln. He described himself as "thunderstruck and stunned." For he saw that, far from being the simple democratic solution that it appeared to be on the surface, popular sovereignty created many more problems. Now the Whigs could no longer hope that slavery would simply die out naturally over time if not allowed to spread. Moreover, the abolitionists and slave owners would now engage in fierce competition to settle the territories and stuff the ballot boxes. Lincoln feared that the Kansas-Nebraska Act would usher in violent confrontations like the one that had killed Elijah Lovejoy nearly 20 years before.

Bleeding Kansas

Lincoln's fears were soon realized. By 1856, the territory of Kansas had become a battle zone. Abolitionists from the North and slave owners from the South recruited settlers to flood the territory, register phony land claims, and rig local elections. The hatred between the two groups flared into hysterical rallies, arson, riots, and murder. Soon, the strife-torn territory gained the nickname "Bleeding Kansas."

The strife reached from Kansas all the way to the nation's capital. On the Senate floor, Senator Charles Sumner of Massachusetts, who was sympathetic to the abolitionist movement, delivered a biting, two-hour speech called "The Crime Against Kansas." He aroused such passion that he was attacked on the spot by Representative Preston Brooks of South Carolina, who bludgeoned him with a heavy cane and injured him severely.

Lincoln was appalled. If elected congressmen could act this way, was there any hope of a peaceful solution for the nation? He himself had not been idle. He had criss-crossed Illinois making speeches against Douglas' popular sovereignty idea and against the "monstrous injustice" of slavery. "I have always thought that all men should be free," he said, "but if any should be slaves, it should be first those who desire it for themselves, and secondly those who desire it for others. Whenever I hear anyone arguing for slavery, I feel a strong impulse to see it tried on him personally."

In 1857 the abolitionist movement suffered a setback when the Supreme Court handed down the Dred Scott decision. The decision was based on the case of a slave named Dred Scott who claimed that he should be freed because his master had twice taken him into free states. But the Supreme Court denied Scott's petition. The Court went on to rule that Congress could not outlaw slavery in any territory because to do so would be to violate the property rights guaranteed by the Constitution. The decision made southerners jubilant, but it only fueled the fires of antislavery protests in the North.

The temper of the times was urgent. Lincoln felt a desperate need to do something to fight the spread of slavery, to halt the growing rift within the country. He wanted the people to shake off what he called "the bear hug of disunion" that was threatening national unity. He ran for the U.S. Senate in 1856 but lost. Later that year he left the Whigs.

The Republican Party

A new political party had begun to form in 1854, largely as a result of the Kansas-Nebraska Act. It began with a group of Whigs who split from their party to take a stronger antislavery stand. Democrats with antislavery feelings also joined the new faction, which was called the Republican Party.

The chief goal of the Republicans was to halt the spread of slavery. Not long after Lincoln joined the Republicans in 1856, the Whig party, which had been unable to agree on a single consistent position on the slavery issue, fractured into a number of small, ineffective splinter groups and then died out. When James Buchanan, a Democrat, was elected President in 1856, the Republicans won some governorships and congressional seats. Now it would be Democrats versus Republicans in every election.

"A House Divided"

In early 1858, the Republican Party in Illinois agreed to nominate Lincoln as its candidate for the U.S. Senate. The Democratic candidate was Douglas, running for re-election. It was clear that the main issue of the campaign would be the spread of slavery.

Lincoln was to deliver the first speech of the campaign at the Republican state convention in Springfield in June. He spent a lot of time on the speech, searching for the words to express his beliefs about slavery and his fears and hopes for the Union. When he delivered it, it was greeted with thunderous applause and cheers.

He delivered versions of the same speech many times during the next few months. It came to be called the "House Divided" speech, after a Bible verse that Lincoln quoted in the speech's most famous passage: " 'A house divided against itself cannot stand.' I believe this government cannot endure, permanently half slave and half free. I do not expect the Union to be dissolved; I do not expect the house to fall; but I do expect it will cease to be divided. It will become all one thing, or all the other."

THE LINCOLN-DOUGLAS DEBATES OF 1858

As Lincoln's campaign progressed, it became more than a contest for a Senate seat from one state; it became a debate that captured the attention and feelings of the whole nation. Lincoln and Douglas argued not just over the question of slavery in the new territories but over the very morality of slavery itself.

The Little Giant

Douglas was a formidable opponent. He was short—a foot shorter than Lincoln—but he was called the "Little Giant" because of his forceful personality, ringing voice, and persuasive speech-making skills. He was stocky, polished, and confident. He was also powerfully ambitious. He had many friends and supporters in Congress and yearned to become President. Next to Douglas, Lincoln looked especially tall and knobby, and his frontier accent seemed intensified. The newspapers dubbed him "Long Abe."

At first, Lincoln and Douglas criss-crossed the state separately. Douglas would roll into a town in his private railroad car, address a rally, and then move on; a day or two later, Lincoln would arrive in the same town in a public railroad car, carrying his notes and books in a worn carpetbag, and attack the points Douglas had made in his speech. In the next town, the process might be reversed. Soon the fiery oratory of the two seized the attention of newspapers in the East. Reporters dogged their steps and telegraph wires hummed after every speech. Finally, the candidates agreed to seven face-to-face debates in August, September, and October.

Every debate spawned a carnival atmosphere, with bands, fireworks, parades, and hordes of supporters wearing

The Lincoln-Douglas debates drew huge crowds and seized the attention of the entire nation. Pitted against the speech-making skills of the "Little Giant," Lincoln delivered his famous speech that claimed, "A house divided against itself cannot stand." (Library of Congress.)

Lincoln or Douglas badges. But at the heart of the hoopla was a deadly serious rivalry that stretched all the way back to the days when Lincoln and Douglas used to argue in front of the fireplace in the back room of Joshua Speed's store.

In spite of their rivalry, Lincoln and Douglas were not all that far apart on some aspects of the slavery issue. Both occupied moderate positions. Lincoln was not an abolitionist. Douglas did not think slavery was a particularly good thing; he just did not have strong feelings against it. The two men really differed on only one crucial point: What was to be done about the spread of slavery into new territories? Lincoln said that it should not be allowed; Douglas continued to promote popular sovereignty, or letting each community decide. This was the point that aroused passionate feelings and passionate words.

Douglas took issue with Lincoln's "House Divided" speech. Why couldn't the nation endure half slave and half free? Let each state decide for itself—wasn't that the democratic way? And was it not ridiculous to talk about the rights of black people? "I believe this government was made by the white man for the white man to be administered by the white man," Douglas asserted. He went on to portray Lincoln as a meddling abolitionist who wanted to free the southern blacks so that they could swarm into the North and cause all kinds of trouble. Maybe Lincoln thought that blacks should be able to vote, Douglas sneered. Maybe he thought they should be allowed to marry whites.

Lincoln was forced to clarify his feelings about the races. He said that he did not believe in full racial equality and that he did believe whites were the superior race. "I have no purpose to introduce political and social equality between the white and the black races," he said. "There is a physical difference between the two, which, in my judgment, will probably forever forbid their living together upon the footing of perfect equality; and inasmuch as it becomes a necessity that there should be a difference, I, as well as Judge Douglas, am in favor of the race to which I belong having the superior position."

Freedom for All

Lincoln went on to say, however, that just because the races were not equal in all ways did not mean that they were not equally entitled to freedom and to "life, liberty, and the pursuit of happiness," as set forth by the founding fathers in the Declaration of Independence. "This government was instituted to secure the blessings of freedom," he reminded his hearers. "Slavery is an unqualified evil to the Negro, to the white man, to the soil, and to the state."

Slavery, he concluded, was just plain wrong. The founders of the country's democratic principles would never have wanted it to spread beyond the places where it existed when the Constitution was drawn up. Popular sovereignty was a mistake for two reasons: because it allowed a moral injustice to grow, and because it meant that citizens and states would have to take sides in a conflict that could threaten national unity.

At the same time, however, Lincoln hastened to point out that he did not want to abolish slavery in the states where it had existed for a long time, although he continued to hope that it would die out there. He simply wanted to keep this great evil, which he compared to a cancer, from infecting the rest of the American body.

The debates stirred tremendous public interest in the election, both in Illinois and across the land. At the time, senators were elected by state legislatures, not by direct vote of the people. When the Illinois legislature cast its ballots, the result was quite close—Lincoln lost to Douglas by two votes. After all his time, energy, and commitment, Lincoln was not to go to the U.S. Senate after all. "I feel like the boy who stumped his toe," he told friends. "I am too big to cry and too badly hurt to laugh."

LINCOLN FOR PRESIDENT

Although he lost the Senate race, Lincoln gained nationwide fame as a result of his debates with Douglas. The national Republican Party began to speak of him as a likely candidate for the presidency in 1860. Lincoln liked the idea and admitted, "The taste *is* in my mouth a little."

In 1859 an event occurred that angered the entire South. A Northern abolitionist named John Brown led an ill-advised raid on a federal weapons storehouse in Harpers Ferry, Virginia. He and his fellow raiders had a confused plan for setting up an independent nation for runaway slaves. They were captured and executed, but the incident caused a sensation. Abolitionists in the North called Brown a hero and martyr and draped their churches in mourning black on the day of his execution. Meanwhile, hysterical southerners accused the North of encouraging a slave revolt.

For the first time, the South began to talk openly of leaving the Union. Jefferson Davis, a senator from Mississippi, said that the raid could lead to "civil war." Lincoln realized that, if he became President, he would have a crisis on his hands. He did not yet know that Davis was right—the crisis would turn into the Civil War.

Chapter 8

The Nation Divided

In May of 1860, Lincoln's "Honest Abe" image was created—without his help—at the state Republican convention, when his relative, John Hanks, and another supporter carried a banner fastened to fence rails they claimed had been split by Lincoln. This homespun pioneer image of the rail-splitting farmer for President appealed to the people, and from then on Lincoln was stuck with it.

THE ELECTION AND AFTERMATH

A few weeks later, Lincoln received the national Republican Party's nomination for President. Other leading Republicans—including William H. Seward of New York, who had hoped for the nomination—gave him their wholehearted support. The race was on. And once again Lincoln's opponent was Stephen A. Douglas, who was running for President with the support of the bulk of the Democratic Party. Two other candidates were sponsored by small parties that had split off from the Democrats.

Lincoln remained at home in Springfield and let others carry on his presidential campaign, as was the custom of the times. But he was busy with correspondence to newspapers, campaign managers, friends, and supporters. Not all his correspondence was serious. He received a letter from an 11-

year-old girl in Westfield, New York, who suggested that he would look handsomer with a beard. Lincoln answered her politely—and then began to grow a beard. He was the first President to wear one.

Election Day

On election day in November of 1860, Lincoln lurked in the telegraph office, anxiously awaiting the election results. Finally, he made his way home through cheering crowds to tell Mary the news. He had carried 18 northern states and won 1,866,452 votes, or 40 percent of the popular votes; and he had won nearly 60 percent of the crucial electoral college vote. Although not one southerner voted for him, Lincoln would be the 16th President. The "Giant Killer," as some newspapers now called him, had finally defeated the Little Giant.

"Well, boys, your troubles are over now," Lincoln told a bunch of newspaper reporters the next day. "Mine have just begun." He was right; trouble was brewing. Even before he took office, Lincoln was faced with the disaster he had feared for so long. The American Union was torn apart.

SECESSION

The southern states viewed Lincoln's election as the death knell of slavery and of their plantation life. Southern leaders had been threatening that the South would secede from the Union. In December, the threat was made good. South Carolina declared itself independent of the United States. Six other states followed in February. As one southern paper proclaimed, "The revolution of 1860 has begun."

Secession—that is, the withdrawal of a state from a larger

confederation, or group of states—was not a brand-new issue in America. The exact nature of the relationship that bound the states together in the Union was nowhere spelled out, not even in the Declaration of Independence or the Constitution. In the Treaty of 1787, which had ended the American Revolution, England acknowledged the independence of "the sovereign states" of North America. This language suggested to many people that each state was really a sovereign nation, with the right to govern itself independently if it chose to do so. Throughout the early years of the United States, the question of states' rights versus the power of the federal (central) government was hammered out bit by bit, in a series of many compromises, laws, and Supreme Court decisions. People took a stand on the issue: one was either a states'-rights man or a believer in a strong federal government. Political parties formed around the question. And over and over again, the states tested the extent of their power.

Some New England states threatened to secede in 1803, when the Louisiana Purchase was made, and again in 1811, when statehood for Louisiana was proposed, because many New Englanders felt that the purchase was unconstitutional and would add slave states to the Union. In 1832 and 1833, during the presidency of Andrew Jackson, a group of South Carolinians who were discontented with the nation's trade taxes led a secession movement in their state; they were thwarted by the President's shrewd combination of firmness and compromise. But the threat of secession remained.

Starting in about 1830, the secession threat was used often by those who disagreed with the policies of the federal government regarding slavery. At first, surprisingly, it was the vehement northern abolitionists who wanted to split the Union. They recommended that the free states secede and form a new nation, leaving the slave states as a separate country. These sentiments died out as the abolitionists felt a growing need to wipe out slavery in the entire nation. By the time of Lincoln's election, the South was on the defensive. For most southerners, secession seemed the only way to survive. But for most northerners, including Lincoln, the Union of *all* the states was a precious thing that could not be destroyed by any of its parts. Secession, in short, was illegal. Unfortunately, Lincoln wasn't sure just what he could do about it.

Farewell to Springfield

On February 11, 1861, Lincoln boarded a train for Washington and his inauguration. He seemed to feel some gloomy foreboding when he told the crowd at the station how sad he was to be leaving Springfield. "Here I have lived a quarter of a century, and have passed from a young to an old man," he said. "Here my children have been born, and one is buried. I now leave, not knowing when, or whether ever, I shall return."

By now, the South was in a fever of unrest. The seven seceding states had formed a new government, which they called the Confederate States of America. They adopted a constitution and named Jefferson Davis of Mississippi as their president. As his train made its way eastward, Lincoln was asked what he would do about the Confederacy. He replied that the Constitution made no provision for secession, and that the formation of the Confederacy was illegal. He expected the South to come to its senses, but if it did not, he would put his foot down "firmly."

So agitated was southern feeling against Lincoln that he received many threats. Chicago detective Allan Pinkerton, convinced that an attempt on Lincoln's life would be made in Baltimore, rode with him on the train to protect him. On Pinkerton's advice, Lincoln sneaked through Baltimore in disguise. He later regretted doing this, for it gave southern papers the opportunity to call him a coward.

An Embattled President

Lincoln's presidency thus began on a note of disunion and discord. Even his inauguration, on March 4, 1861, had an embattled look: army riflemen were posted on rooftops along the parade route and at the windows of the Capitol in case violence broke out. Lincoln took the oath of office and then made a speech in which he called upon the South to abandon its revolution. But he promised not to attack the Confederacy unless in defense. "In your hands, my dissatisfied fellow countrymen, and not in mine, is the momentous issue of civil war," he declared. "You can have no conflict, without being yourselves the aggressors."

THE WAR BEGINS

Lincoln quickly assembled his Cabinet: William Seward of New York as secretary of state; Salmon P. Chase of Ohio as secretary of the treasury (Lincoln appointed him to the Supreme Court in 1864); Simon Cameron of Pennsylvania as secretary of war; Edward Bates of Missouri as attorney general (in 1864, Lincoln replaced Bates with James Speed, Joshua's brother); Gideon Welles of Connecticut as secretary of the Navy (he introduced ironclad ships, including the famous *Monitor*); Montgomery Blair of Maryland as postmaster general (Blair was moderate in his views and became so unpopular with proabolitionist Republicans that Lincoln was forced to replace him in 1864 with William Dennison of Indiana); and Caleb B. Smith of Indiana as secretary of the interior (he became a judge in 1863 and was replaced with John P. Usher).

Of course, Lincoln did not give Douglas, his Democratic opponent, a Cabinet seat. But because Douglas did not agree with the South's secession, he nevertheless vowed to support the new President. Douglas thereupon embarked on a speak-

The Confederate shelling of Fort Sumter, a Union fort in the harbor of Charleston, South Carolina, marked the start of the Civil War. Before that war ended, it would cost as many lives as the United States has lost in all its other wars combined. (Library of Congress.)

ing tour to rally northern Democrats behind Lincoln, but he died only a few weeks later of typhoid fever.

With his Cabinet and his military advisors, Lincoln struggled to find a solution to the secession problem, but the South refused to compromise. Lincoln offered to continue to allow slavery in the original slave states, but the Confederacy now insisted that slavery be made legal everywhere. This Lincoln would not permit. The time for negotiation, it appeared, was over.

Fort Sumter

On April 12, 1861, the first shot of the Civil War was fired by Confederate cannon in the harbor of Charleston, South Carolina. The Confederates attacked Union ships that Lincoln had ordered to carry supplies to Fort Sumter, a Union military post at the harbor's entrance. The governor of South Carolina had requested Lincoln to give the fort up, but he would not do so.

Then, because the fort refused to surrender, the Confederates began shelling it. Two days later, after 36 hours of bombing, Fort Sumter surrendered. That same day, Lincoln called for 75,000 volunteers to enlist for 90 days. Surely, he felt, the rebellion could be stamped out in three months.

Eleven states had now joined the Confederacy (Alabama, Arkansas, Florida, Georgia, Louisiana, Mississippi, North Carolina, South Carolina, Tennessee, Texas, and Virginia). But the North had 23 states, including the so-called "border states"—that is, the slave states of Delaware, Maryland, Kentucky, and Missouri, which remained loyal to the Union. The North had 22 million people against the South's nine million, one third of whom were slaves. The North also had most of the nation's money, factories, railroads, and naval vessels.

What did the South have to offset these advantages? Military talent. Robert E. Lee of Virginia was probably the finest general of his time. Lincoln offered him the command of the Union army, but instead he accepted command of the Confederate forces. Other Confederate officers were equally brilliant.

When the Confederate capital was moved to Richmond, Virginia, in June of 1861, the Union's Army of the Potomac, under the command of General Irwin McDowell, began massing for an attack on Richmond. On July 21, as Lincoln sat in his office in the White House, watching the wind snap the Confederate flags that flew over Alexandria, Virginia, just across the Potomac River, McDowell's army began its march toward Richmond. "On to Richmond!" was the confident Union battle cry.

Bull Run

A 24,000-man Confederate army advanced northward against McDowell's 30,000 troops. Word reached Washington that the two forces were going to meet at a small, muddy creek called Bull Run, near Manassas Junction, Virginia. The Union soldiers were light-hearted as they marched toward the battlefield. They sang, picked blueberries, and joked about how they'd be home before sundown.

The light-hearted mood infected Washington, too. Newspapermen, politicians and their wives, and others who were eager to observe the battle arrived on the scene by the hundreds. Carrying picnic hampers, bottles of champagne, and opera glasses, they settled themselves on the surrounding hillsides like spectators at a play.

The play turned out to be a tragedy. Confederate General Thomas J. Jackson held his troops so firmly against the Union advance that he was called "Stonewall" Jackson ever after. The horrified Union spectators saw their army halted in its tracks, mowed down by gunfire and lacerated by slashing bayonets wielded by yelling Confederate troops.

McDowell's forces had to retreat, and the retreat soon became a panic, with soldiers dropping their weapons and fleeing madly northward, mixed in with the lathered horses and rocking carriages of the terrified civilians. As the next day's dawn broke, a heartsick President Lincoln saw his beaten and disorderly army come limping back into the capital.

That first battle of the Civil War was called Bull Run in the North, Manassas in the South. Under either name, it changed everyone's thinking about the war. Although they had lost 2,000 men, the Confederates gained the enormous psychological thrill of the first victory. And to the Union, which had lost 3,000 men, the battle brought the agonizing realization that this was not going to be an easy war to win. For Lincoln, the conflict that he had confidently assumed would be over in three months had, instead, turned into a nightmare that seemed never-ending.

Commander-in-Chief

With no military training or experience, Lincoln suddenly found himself the Commander-in-Chief of a force engaged in a desperate struggle to preserve the very existence of the United States. He was all too aware of his own lack of military skill, and he knew that he needed generals upon whom he could rely. But he had bad luck with a number of his military commanders. The course of the war, in fact, would be marked by Lincoln's attempts to find a general who would take the offensive and *fight*.

At first, Lincoln followed the advice of General Winfield Scott, the general-in-chief of all the Union armies. But Scott was 75 years old and ill; he fell asleep during planning meetings. Lincoln soon lost confidence in him and pinned his hopes on George B. McClellan, a dapper young general from the Mexican-American War. But McClellan, too, was a disappointment. Although he had enlisted nearly 200,000 soldiers by November of 1861, he did not march on the South as Lincoln expected. "I need more time," McClellan kept telling the impatient President.

Lincoln decided to take a more active role in directing his armies. He gathered up an armful of books on military strategy and retired to his office, determined to teach himself warfare as he had taught himself surveying and law. He was plagued with problems in the War Department, too. Secretary of War Simon Cameron was revealed as a corrupt administrator who defined an honest politician as one "who when he's bought, stays bought." In 1862, Lincoln replaced him with Edwin M. Stanton of Ohio. Stanton, Seward, and Chase eventually became the President's friends as well as his Cabinet advisors.

TROUBLE ON ALL SIDES

Because he was being criticized by many people for not having been able to end the war quickly, Lincoln needed friends as he entered the second year of his presidency. Some northern Democrats called Lincoln a warmonger and demanded that he make a truce with the South (these "peace Democrats" were nicknamed Copperheads, after the poisonous snake of that name). McClellan was still dragging his feet about taking the Army of the Potomac into the South, and because enlistment in the army was down, for the first time the country had to have a draft to obtain more military manpower. On top of everything else, Lincoln suffered a crushing personal loss in early 1862.

During 1861, Lincoln relaxed whenever he could by playing for an hour or two with Willie and Taddie (Robert, his oldest son, was away at Harvard University, in Massachusetts). Both boys, the first young children of a President to live in the White House, fell ill in February. Taddie recovered, but

11-year-old Willie died. Lincoln had adored this solemn, quiet boy who loved to read and write poetry and was thoughtful and intelligent.

Willie's death deeply sorrowed Lincoln. But it almost unhinged Mary, who wept inconsolably and did not leave her room for three months. She never fully recovered from the effects of her grief, and afterward she was nervous, reclusive, jealous of other people around Lincoln, and somewhat unpredictable in behavior.

At some point Mary experimented with spiritualism, meeting with mediums who claimed to be able to communicate with Willie's spirit. She also tried to soothe her unhappiness with shopping trips to New York, but her spending became uncontrollable. In one three-month period she bought more than 300 pairs of gloves. She accumulated debts of more than $27,000, which she tried desperately to keep secret from her husband, and the guilt she felt about this preyed on her mind.

The war brought Mary further suffering, too. Many of her closest relatives chose the Confederate side; some of them were killed in the fighting. Although Lincoln's enemies accused her of being a Confederate sympathizer, or even a spy, these charges were utterly untrue. Even though she no longer took an interest in the day-to-day details of Lincoln's political actions, she was completely supportive of the Union and of his policies.

War in the West

Lincoln buried his grief over Willie's death in work. He was more committed than ever to preserving the Union, and he resolved to conduct the war in the way that he thought was right, regardless of criticism.

Some of Lincoln's war policies were harsh and extremely

unpopular; in fact, there were times when he was one of the most unpopular Presidents the country has ever had. In 1862 he imposed martial law (military law) in the country. This allowed the army to imprison without trial anyone believed to be a traitor to the Union cause. Altogether, more than 13,000 people were jailed under martial law. A few of them really were traitors, but many were simply people who disagreed with Lincoln or wanted peace at any cost. Most were soon released.

In the meantime, the war raged on. Lincoln and his advisors spent long days and nights in the war room of the White House studying or writing dispatches, marking the advances of various armies on huge maps, and waiting for telegrams bringing news of battles.

Early in 1862 the Union won some important victories in the West: Missouri, Kentucky, and Tennessee. In February, General Ulysses S. Grant captured a Confederate outpost in Tennessee called Fort Donelson. Grant's message to the commanding Confederate officer was: "No terms but immediate and unconditional surrender." "Unconditional Surrender" Grant, as he was dubbed, became the Union's hero.

In April, Grant's troops were caught unawares by a surprise attack at Shiloh, in southwestern Tennessee. Although unprepared, the Union soldiers stood fast. The battle was the worst the nation had known up to that time—about 24,000 men were killed in a smoky, roaring melee. Many of them were young boys, barely trained to fight. Elsewhere in the West, the Union seized and held Confederate territory: New Orleans, Baton Rouge, and much of the Mississippi River Valley. This was welcome news, for back in the East, the Army of the Potomac was in trouble.

Chapter 9

War and Emancipation

Everyone knew that the war would be won or lost, not on the western frontier, but in the East. But Lincoln despaired of getting McClellan to move. Finally, in early 1862, the President ordered the Army of the Potomac to advance south on Richmond. McClellan moved 100,000 men by sea to a position south of Richmond on the Virginia shore. His march on the Confederate capital was so slow, however, that Confederate forces were able to gather in sufficient strength to hold him off. Disgusted with McClellan's tardiness, Lincoln replaced him with Henry Halleck as general-in-chief and John Pope as general of the Army of the Potomac.

After McClellan's failed assault on Richmond, the Confederate army moved north under Lee and dealt Pope's army a stinging defeat at the Second Battle of Bull Run in August. The Confederates then continued north into Maryland. Desperate to halt their advance, Lincoln fired Pope and reinstated McClellan. Lee and McClellan then fought a bloody battle at Antietam Creek in Maryland in September. The Confederates were turned back, but McClellan did not pursue Lee's army, and it was able to escape across the Potomac River into Virginia. Many military historians today agree that the

After the Battle of Antietam, Lincoln visited General McClellan (seated on right) in his headquarters on the battlefield. Lincoln was furious with McClellan for not pursuing and destroying General Lee's retreating Confederate army—which might have ended the war. A few weeks later, Lincoln relieved McClellan of his command. (Library of Congress.)

Union could have won the war after Antietam if McClellan had pursued and attacked Lee.

By this time Lincoln was exasperated almost beyond measure. He wanted the Army of the Potomac to attack and smash Lee's army, not just to block its advances. Irritated with what he called McClellan's "slows," the President peppered his general with snappy telegrams. One read: "If you don't want to use the army, I should like to borrow it for a while." Another said: "I have just read your dispatch about sore-tongued and fatigued horses. Will you pardon me for asking what the horses of your army have done since the battle of Antietam that fatigues anything?" In November, Lincoln once again relieved McClellan of his command and replaced him with General Ambrose E. Burnside.

Fredericksburg and Chancellorsville

Burnside led the Army of the Potomac to Fredericksburg, Virginia, where he engaged Lee in battle in December of 1862. But instead of being the victory Lincoln had hoped for, the Battle of Fredericksburg was a disaster. While Burnside's men were busy building bridges to carry them across the Rappahannock River, Lee's riflemen raked them with savage fire. By the time Burnside retreated, he had lost 12,000 men. Knowing what Lincoln's reaction would be, he resigned his command.

Lincoln's next choice to lead the Army of the Potomac was General Joseph "Fighting Joe" Hooker. When he took command, Hooker announced a campaign against Richmond: "My plans are perfect, and when I carry them out, may God have mercy on General Lee, for I will have none." But Hooker was over-confident. He met Lee—who had only half as many men—at Chancellorsville, Virginia, in May of 1863. The Confederate troops hammered Hooker's larger army, killing thousands of men and forcing Hooker to retreat ingloriously. Victory was costly, though. Lee lost 12,000 men at Chancellorsville—including General Stonewall Jackson, who was accidentally shot and killed by his own men.

Once again, Lincoln looked about for someone—anyone—to lead the Army of the Potomac capably. He then decided upon General George G. Meade, who no sooner had taken command of the army than he received word that Lee was once more heading north. Just as after the Second Battle of Bull Run, Lee seemed to be heading for central Penn-

Civil War Cameraman

The people and events of Lincoln's presidency—and especially of the Civil War— have been preserved for us in hundreds of photographs. Lincoln's life and presidential administration are better illustrated than any earlier period in history, thanks to the skill and energy of Mathew Brady, perhaps America's most famous photographer.

Brady was born sometime around 1823 in the Lake George region of New York State. As a young man, he was introduced to Samuel F. B. Morse, a well-known artist who later invented the telegraph. Morse's interests included the brand-new art of photography. He taught young Brady to take daguerreo-types, as the early photographs were called (in honor of the Frenchman L. J. M. Daguerre, who had pioneered the most widely used photographic process in the 1820s). Because of Brady's great skill with the camera, the public became enchanted with this new way of making portraits. Brady prospered and was able to open a studio and gallery in New York City in 1844.

A year later, Brady embarked on an ambi-tious plan to photograph all the great men and women of his time. Many of his da-guerreotypes survive, carrying the images of famous people—and some not-so-famous ones—down through the years. One of his most important achievements was his presidential series, which includes portraits of every President from John Quincy Adams (the

sixth) to William McKinley (the 25th); the
only exception is William Henry Harrison.

Unlike modern photographs, early daguerreotypes required the subjects to sit very still
in front of the camera for several seconds. As
a result, surviving images of 19th-century
people usually have a stiff, posed look rather
than the natural, active photographs of today.
In addition, daguerreotypes were something
of a luxury. People tended to have their pic-
tures taken in formal dress and on formal oc-
casions, not to capture scenes from their
everyday lives. Nevertheless, these old daguerreotypes do more than tell us about the past—
they let us look at it through a window.

When the Civil War broke out, Brady
decided to do something that had never been
done before. He wanted to make a complete
pictorial record of this titanic conflict. He
spent his personal fortune of $100,000 hiring
teams of photographers and supplying them
with cameras and other equipment. Under his
direction, these photographers covered camps
and battlefields from Virginia to Missouri. In
many ways, they were the forerunners of today's newsphoto services. Brady himself pho-
tographed the First Battle of Bull Run, the
Battle of Antietam, the Battle of Fredericksburg, and the battlefield at Gettysburg. He
came under fire while taking daguerreotypes
at Petersburg, Virginia, in 1864. He also took
a number of memorable portraits of Lincoln
and a famous portrait of defeated Confederate General Robert E. Lee.

Among Mathew Brady's achievements in photographing the Civil War is this picture of the Battle of Antietam. One of the very few action shots taken of the conflict, it shows a line of Union artillery (across the middle of the picture) firing on the Confederates. (Library of Congress.)

The cost of photographing the war drained Brady's fortune. Plagued by debts, he went bankrupt, and in 1874 his photographic plates were sold at public auction. The War Department bought the plates for $2,840, and eventually, Congress gave Brady a grant of $25,000. Brady tried to revive his business with a gallery in Washington, D.C., but by now he had many competitors, and he did not do as well as in his early days.

Mathew Brady died, alone and forgotten, in the paupers' ward of a New York City hospital in 1896. But in his hundreds of daguerreotypes, he left a priceless record of 19th-century America.

sylvania. Meade hurried to stop him. The result was the Battle of Gettysburg, the bloodiest battle of the Civil War—or, indeed, of American history. And once again, after the battle, the Union failed to seize the advantage. Lee slipped away, as he had done after Antietam. Lincoln had been let down by another general.

THE EMANCIPATION PROCLAMATION

To most people, Lincoln's presidency is synonymous with the Civil War. And it is true that the war dominated Lincoln's administration in a way that no other single event has absorbed a presidency. Foreign relations were neglected—except for the masterful jobs done by Secretary of State William Seward and the ambassador to England, Charles Francis Adams (son of President John Quincy Adams and grandson of President John Adams). These two men were able to keep the English from recognizing and aiding the Confederate States of America. All other political activities at home and abroad took second place to the urgencies of the war.

Nevertheless, Lincoln's administration contained some significant events. In 1862 Congress passed the Homestead Act, which opened up vast tracts of public land—mostly in the West—to farmers and settlers, who could obtain title to 160 acres simply by living and working on the land. West Virginia broke off from Virginia and was admitted to the Union (as a slave state) in 1863; Nevada was admitted in 1864. But the political act for which Lincoln is most remembered was directly related to the war. It was the emancipation— that is, the setting free—of the slaves.

What Lincoln Really Did

There is no doubt that Lincoln's personal devotion to the cause of universal freedom was deep and genuine. Yet his emancipation of the slaves is often misunderstood. It was an act not just of philosophical conviction but also of shrewd political judgment.

Initially, Lincoln did not agree with the abolitionists. He had promised to leave slavery alone in the original slave states, and he hoped that this promise would help reconcile the North and the South. In addition, he wanted to keep the loyalty of the border states, so he took no action concerning slavery. He still hoped that the slaves could be freed gradually, over time, and resettled outside the United States.

Many abolitionists became angry with Lincoln for his moderate position. Frederick Douglass accused him of being devoted solely to the white man's interests. In August of 1862, Horace Greeley, a New England newspaper editor, appealed to the President to free at least the slaves of those Confeder-

ates who were fighting the Union. Lincoln replied: "My para-
mount object in this struggle is to save the Union, and is not
either to save or to destroy slavery. If I could save the Union
without freeing any slave I would do it, and if I could save
it by freeing all the slaves I would do it; and if I could do
it by freeing some and leaving others alone I would also do
that." In short, despite the myths that have grown up around
Lincoln, he did not enter the Civil War to free the slaves.
His goal was to keep the Union together by any means.

As the war went on, however, two things made Lincoln
change his mind. First, the Union was desperately short of
soldiers. As parts of the South came under Union control,
many of the slaves in these regions were eager to fight on
the Union side. Some of his advisors urged Lincoln to pro-
claim them free, so that they could enlist (free northern blacks
formed several army companies, too; although they were com-
manded by white officers and not integrated with white soldiers, they fought bravely and with distinction). The second
thing that made Lincoln change his mind about emancipation was the realization that the South was not prepared to
compromise or reconcile with the North. Nothing he could
say or do would make the Confederacy change its course now.

At this point, Lincoln was bombarded with antislavery
appeals from abolitionists, free northern blacks, liberal Republicans like Charles Sumner, and even some northern Democrats. After the Battle of Antietam in September of 1862,
Lincoln decided that, as long as the South was bent on total
war, there was no point in keeping his earlier promise. He
could now do what he really believed was right: he could
free the slaves. His only concern now was to avoid turning
the border states against the Union. So, in a preliminary an-
nouncement about emancipation, he said that on January 1,
1863, he would set free all slaves in all states that were in
rebellion against the Union on that date.

Many escaped slaves were eager to fight in the Union army. One reason for the emancipation of the slaves was to allow them to enlist; they were welcome, as the Union army was growing desperately short of manpower. Free blacks from northern states also fought with distinction in the war. (Library of Congress.)

Jubilation and Anger

A New Year's reception was held in the White House on the morning of January 1. Mary appeared, wearing flowers in her hair; it was her first public appearance since Willie's death. Lincoln greeted visitors and shook hands. At one point, he slipped quietly away to his office. There, attended by members of his Cabinet, he signed his full name to the formal document called the Emancipation Proclamation. "If my name ever goes down in history," he remarked as he signed, "it will be for this act."

Abolitionists rejoiced. Douglass reversed his harsh opinion of Lincoln and wrote, "We shout for joy that we live to record this righteous decree." Hannah Johnson, a black woman in New York whose son was a Union soldier, wrote the President, "When you are dead and in Heaven, in a thousand years that action of yours will make the Angels sing your praise."

Not everyone was happy about the Emancipation Proclamation, however. Lincoln was horrified when, in the summer of 1863, riots broke out in New York City. Citizens objected to being drafted to fight a war "to free the slaves." An armed mob burned the draft office, assaulted the mayor's house, and killed hundreds of people in the city's black district. And across the North, "peace Democrats" were outraged. They did not want slavery abolished; they wanted the nation restored to its pre-war status. One Democratic paper claimed that the proclamation was "wicked, atrocious, and revolting." Some people urged Lincoln to withdraw it, to which he replied, "I am a slow walker, but I never walk backward."

Although Lincoln is called the Great Emancipator, the Emancipation Proclamation did not free all the slaves. It did not free slaves in the border states, and it did not effectively free slaves in the Confederate states, where it could not be enforced. But it did free about 200,000 slaves in Confederate territory that passed into Union hands. And, most of all, it resolved the issue that had been hanging over the nation for decades.

Eventually everyone, including the Copperheads and the slave owners in the border states, realized that slavery was a thing of the past that could not and would not return. Lincoln deserves to be called the Great Emancipator because his Emancipation Proclamation paved the way for the 13th Amendment, which he shepherded through Congress later in his administration. That amendment guaranteed freedom to *all* Americans, black and white, under the Constitution of the United States.

Chapter 10

The End of the Struggle

The war was taking a terrible toll on Lincoln. Photographic portraits taken from 1861 to 1864 show how he aged in office: his hair and beard grew grayer, his cheeks more sunken and gaunt, his eyes bracketed by deep lines of worry and sorrow. He worked for many hours every day, for months without a break. And he was often unwell.

Some doctors today suggest that Lincoln had Marfan's Syndrome, a hereditary disease that affects the bones and heart. Lincoln had the long limbs and sunken chest typical of Marfan's sufferers; he also complained, as they do, of cold hands and feet. If he did have Marfan's Syndrome, he may have been ill with heart disease in the White House. Certainly he was under extreme stress. And he was beset by the agonizing doubts that any leader in his place would have felt: Am I doing the right thing? Is this the best course for the Union? Is there no way to end the killing?

The deaths of so many thousands of men—on both sides—were a great burden of grief. In 1864, Lincoln wrote to one Massachusetts woman who lost several sons, "I know how weak and fruitless must be any word of mine . . . But I cannot refrain from tendering you the consolation that may be found in the thanks of the republic they died to save." By now, thousands of wives and mothers had sacrificed their menfolk on what Lincoln called "the altar of freedom." At times, late at night while he paced the corridors or sat up alone in the White House, he wondered whether their sacrifices would be rewarded, whether the war would ever end.

Lincoln snatched moments of relief from the pressures of his office with his family whenever he could. He tried to spend time with Taddie, who found the White House lonely and sad after Willie's death. And in spite of Mary's occasional difficult moods, his feelings for her remained affectionate and protective. He was sometimes able to arrange for the two of them to escape for a day or so from the sweltering heat or noise of the capital to the Retired Soldier's Home, a comfortable residence in the woods north of Washington. Mary sometimes stayed there for several weeks, while Lincoln rode out each night from his office.

Robert graduated from Harvard in 1864. Although Lincoln had never been as close to Robert as to his younger boys, he was proud of his son and enjoyed his company. But many people wondered why Robert was not fighting at a time when other families had to watch their sons and brothers march off to war. For a long time Mary refused to consider the possibility; if Robert should be killed, she would have lost three sons. But Robert wanted to enlist and finally, in late 1864, Lincoln overruled Mary's objections. Robert joined the army and received a captain's commission.

THE FINAL MONTHS

The aftermath of the Battle of Gettysburg filled Lincoln with despair. Once again, as at Antietam, the Union had an opportunity to follow Lee, crush his retreating army, and end the war—but failed to do so. Lincoln vowed that it would not happen again.

At the same time, news from the western front was encouraging. On the day Lee's army crept away from Gettysburg—July 4, 1863—General Grant accepted the surrender of Vicksburg, Mississippi. Vicksburg was the last big Confederate base on the river; now the entire Mississippi Valley was in Union hands.

Lincoln had been impressed with Grant ever since his capture of Fort Donelson. The tough-talking, cigar-chomping Ohioan was the only one of Lincoln's generals who seemed eager and able to attack, attack, attack. He didn't always follow orders, but he always got results.

When advisors urged Lincoln to get rid of Grant because he had been taken by surprise at Shiloh, Lincoln replied, "I can't spare this man. He fights." And when critics raised old charges of drunkenness against Grant and accused him of drinking whiskey during military actions, Lincoln retorted with a touch of impatience, "Find out the name of his brand so I can give it to my other generals."

Following Vicksburg, Grant led his army doggedly through Tennessee, winning a notable victory at Chattanooga in November, about a week after Lincoln delivered his address at Gettysburg. Lincoln decided that here was the commander who could win the war. He called Grant to Washington and early in 1864 named him general-in-chief of all Union armies.

Grant and Sherman

Together, Lincoln and Grant worked out a plan. The Union would launch a simultaneous attack against the Confederacy's two strong men: Lee in Virginia and General Joseph Johnston in the Georgia-Tennessee region. Grant would drive south with 115,000 men to attack Lee at Richmond. At the same time, General William Tecumseh Sherman, who had been leading Union forces in Tennessee, would advance with

100,000 men toward Johnston and the Confederate stronghold of Atlanta, Georgia, which was an important railroad center and held stockpiles of grain and other supplies.

In May, the offensive began. Grant crossed the Rapidan River into Virginia. There, in a rugged area of swamps, hills, and dense forests called The Wilderness, he ran into Lee's army. The Wilderness campaign became a bloody, inch-by-inch conflict that went on for months. Lee put up such a stubborn resistance that Grant's losses were staggering. In countless skirmishes in the woods and in three major battles near Richmond, Grant lost 54,000 men. But he refused to retreat, and he refused to give up the attack. "I propose to fight it out on these lines if it takes all summer," he telegraphed to Lincoln.

Grant's campaign did take all summer, and beyond. The Union death toll mounted higher and higher. The newspapers printed long lists of the casualties, and every day steamers unloaded shiploads of Union dead and wounded on northern wharves. The slaughter now seemed to many in the North to be senseless and inhuman, and the antiwar movement gained strength.

Meantime, farther South, Sherman also was encountering strong resistance by Johnston's army. But in September, Sherman broke through. His army then marched on Atlanta, sacked and burned that city (events that are colorfully portrayed in the famous book and movie, *Gone With the Wind*), and continued its advance through Georgia to the coastal city of Savannah. Sherman was a believer in what is sometimes called "total war." He said, "We are not only fighting hostile armies, but a hostile people, and must make old and young, rich and poor, feel the hard hand of war." During his notorious "march to the sea," Sherman's army burned homes and farms, destroyed crops, killed or scattered livestock, and generally left a path of ruin and destruction.

Sherman's march through Georgia demoralized and crippled the Deep South. It also turned the tide of war for the Union. For Lincoln, the upturn in Union fortunes came just in time.

THE ELECTION OF 1864

In the midst of carrying on the war, Lincoln had to worry about re-election in 1864. Seeking to build as wide a base of support as possible, the Republican Party temporarily called itself the National Union Party so that it could include the "war Democrats"– that is, Democrats who approved of the President's conduct of the war and might be expected to vote for him.

At the national party convention in June, Lincoln was renominated. His Vice-President, Hannibal Hamlin of Maine, expected renomination as well. But Lincoln dropped Hamlin in favor of Andrew Johnson, a Democrat from Tennessee who had remained loyal to the Union. This way, he felt, his campaign would draw voters from both Republican and Democratic parties.

Lincoln's opponent was none other than his former general-in-chief, George B. McClellan, running as the candidate of the "peace Democrats." McClellan blasted Lincoln as a bad wartime commander and proposed an immediate truce with the South.

As the summer of 1864 wore on, Lincoln's prospects for re-election looked dim because the war was going badly. In July, a Confederate force under General Jubal Early made a daring raid into Maryland and reached a point just two miles from Washington before it was turned back. Early's force escaped into Virginia, loaded with stolen supplies. Grant was bogged down in The Wilderness campaign; Sherman was stymied in Georgia. Thousands of men were dying every month, and the end seemed nowhere in sight. The country was tired of the killing, tired of the war—and tired of Lincoln, too. In August, the discouraged President wrote in a private note that "it seems exceedingly probable that this administration will not be re-elected."

But Sherman captured Atlanta on September 1, and soon afterward Union Admiral David G. Farragut destroyed the Confederate navy in Mobile Bay, Alabama. In Virginia, Grant dug in outside Richmond and waited for Sherman to sweep up from Georgia to help him take the Confederate capital. Now it appeared that the end of the war was in sight after all—and it would be a Union victory. On election day in November, the voters demonstrated their restored confidence in Lincoln. He received 2,213,635 popular votes to McClellan's 1,805,237 and 212 electoral votes to his 21. Lincoln received almost all of the soldiers' votes.

"With Malice Toward None, With Charity Toward All"

On March 4, 1865, Lincoln delivered his second inaugural address, one of the greatest speeches he ever made. In it, he rejoiced that slavery had been abolished forever in the United States (Congress had passed the 13th Amendment in January). The "mighty scourge of war," Lincoln said, was the nation's punishment for having allowed slavery to continue. But now it was over. Soon it would be time to reunite and rebuild. And it was vitally important, Lincoln told his listeners, that there be no lasting bitterness between North and South:

> With malice toward none, with charity toward all, with firmness in the right as God gives us to see the right, let us strive on to finish the work we are in, to bind up the nation's wounds, to care for him who shall have borne the battle and for his widow and orphan, to do all which may achieve and cherish a just and lasting peace among ourselves and with all nations.

Lincoln's first four years as President had been an unrelieved nightmare of war. He looked forward now to a second four years of constructive work, an opportunity to heal and mend, "to bind up the nation's wounds." Tragically, he was not to have that opportunity.

TRIUMPH AND TRAGEDY

The month of April 1865 was one of the most momentous in American history. In that month, Grant broke through Lee's defensive line at Petersburg, not far from Richmond, and swept toward the Confederate capital. Jefferson Davis and other southerners fled, setting fire to bridges behind them to halt pursuit. The wind carried the flames to buildings, and Richmond burned. Lincoln came to the ravaged city the following day and picked his way through the smoldering rubble to Davis' executive mansion, now abandoned—like the hopes of the Confederacy.

A few days later, on April 9, in the parlor of a house in Appomattox, Virginia, General Robert E. Lee surrendered to General Ulysses S. Grant. Robert Todd Lincoln was present as Grant's adjutant, or aide. He watched as the two men— Lee in his full-dress Confederate uniform, complete with jeweled sword, and Grant in a stained and muddy Union field uniform—discussed the terms of the surrender and then respectfully shook hands.

The Civil War, the only war that has pitted Americans against their countrymen, was over after four years. A total of four million troops had fought in it. More than 375,000 of them were wounded and more than 617,000 killed—about the same as the total number of deaths in the American Revolution, the War of 1812, the Spanish-American War, World War I, World War II, the Korean War, and the Vietnam War combined.

The war might have dragged on even longer, with a still greater death toll, for the South was determined to go on fighting as long as it had the strength. But a successful blockade by the Union navy throughout most of the war prevented desperately needed foreign trade and supplies from reaching southern ports. By cutting off the South from the rest of the world, the blockade hastened the war's end.

The First Modern War

The Civil War has been called the world's first modern, or total, war. This means that its outcome was determined by the industrial power and productivity of the North, rather than by the valor of either side's fighting men. In other words, the war was fought everywhere in the land, not just on the battlefields.

One reason the South lost was because it was starving. There was some food, but there were no railroads to carry it to the people. Before the war, the South had fewer rail lines than the North. And when these wore out or were damaged during the war, the South did not have iron foundries to make rails to repair them.

In addition, the South lacked munitions factories, while the North had many of them. The Civil War saw the first military use of machine guns, small-caliber guns that could be handled by one man and were capable of firing up to 3,000 rounds a minute without being reloaded. Nearly a dozen different kinds of machine guns were used by both sides, but the most effective ones — including the Gatling gun — were invented by northerners, manufactured in northern factories, and used by northern soldiers. Military historians attribute the Union victory in part to this superior use of technology.

Before the Civil War, warfare was sometimes thought

of as a kind of game, governed by age-old rules of chivalry. Like the soldiers who picked flowers on the way to the First Battle of Bull Run, or the politicians and their families who gaily carried picnic baskets to that first battlefield, many Americans failed to recognize the seriousness of war or to foresee its consequences. But the Civil War, far vaster in its scope and destruction than any previous American war, changed the rules of warfare. It introduced a new—and, perhaps, more brutal—era, one in which war is a matter not just for armies but for entire nations.

Celebration at Last

Flags flew and bells rang across the North in celebration of the war's end. On the night of April 11, a crowd gathered on the White House lawn to hear the President speak from a window about the great task that lay ahead: the task of reconstruction. On his orders, the defeated southerners were allowed to keep their horses for plowing, their guns for hunting. Let them renew their loyalty to the Union, he declared, and build a new way of life without slaves.

No one knows much about the President's plans for national reconstruction. He left some notes, and, of course, he had talked over the coming problems with Cabinet members and friends. For one thing, he insisted that there be no war trials or executions of any former Confederates—they were all members of the same nation again. But before reconstruction could get under way, Lincoln was no longer President.

Tragedy at Ford's Theatre

At last, the torment of the war was over; the 13th Amendment had been accepted, ending slavery; Lincoln was safely re-elected. And it was spring, the loveliest season of the year

John Wilkes Booth's dramatic leap to the stage after shooting the President caused him to break his ankle. Nevertheless, Booth succeeded in escaping, only to be tracked down and killed a few weeks later. (Library of Congress.)

in Washington, with lilacs and dogwoods in sweet-scented bloom. Little wonder that the President felt he had earned some relaxation.

On April 14, less than a week after Lee's surrender, the Lincolns and another couple attended a performance of the play *Our American Cousin* at Ford's Theatre. They entered the theater to an ovation from the audience and sat in a special presidential box that was hung with flags. Suddenly, during the third act, a shot rang out from the presidential box.

John Wilkes Booth, a slender, dark-haired actor, stood behind the President's seat with a gun in his hand. The confused audience thought for a moment that the interruption was part of the play. Then someone screamed, "The President has been shot!"

Booth leaped from the box onto the stage, but he caught his foot in one of the flags and tripped, breaking his shinbone. He cried out, "*Sic temper tyrannis!*" (Latin for "Thus to all tyrants") and hobbled from the stage to the alley, where a horse was waiting.

The bullet had entered Lincoln's head, but he was not dead. Unconscious, he was carried across the street to a boardinghouse. There he was placed on a bed—diagonally, because of his great height. Vice-President Johnson was notified; he must now prepare himself to take over the government. Friends and Cabinet members rushed to Lincoln's bedside (but not Secretary of State Seward, who had been injured in an unsuccessful assassination attempt by one of Booth's co-conspirators). Mary sobbed and begged the President to speak to her; she grew so hysterical with shock and grief that, finally, she was gently removed from the room.

At about 7:30 the following morning, Lincoln died without regaining consciousness. He was 56 years old. He was also the first American President to be assassinated.

A Nation Mourns

This ghastly event, coming as it did on the heels of Lee's surrender, stunned the nation. A manhunt was mounted for Booth and those who had joined him in the ill-judged plan to kill the key men in Lincoln's administration. Booth, it turned out, was passionately sympathetic to the southern cause; some historians believe that he was also emotionally or mentally disturbed. On April 26, he was killed in a shoot-out with federal troops who had tracked him to a barn in Virginia. Jeffer-

In the Lincoln Memorial in Washington, D.C., this statue of Lincoln, whose grave face and deep-sunk eyes suggest brooding thought, gazes out over the nation's capital. A marble panel in the memorial is inscribed with Lincoln's Gettysburg Address. (Library of Congress.)

son Davis, the former Confederate president, spoke for the many southerners who respected Lincoln and were deeply ashamed of Booth when he said, "Next to the destruction of the Confederacy, the death of Abraham Lincoln was the darkest day the South has ever known."

By then, Lincoln was on his way home to Springfield. His funeral was held in the East Room of the White House on April 19. Afterward, his body was carried in a mournful procession to the rotunda of the United States Capitol building. There it lay in state for a day. Thousands of soldiers and civilians, blacks and whites, lined up in the rain and filed past the coffin to pay their last respects to the preserver of the Union and the Great Emancipator.

Lincoln's body was carried back to Springfield in a special train that was draped with black cloths and bore his portrait, wreathed in flowers, on the engine. It followed the same 1,600-mile route that Lincoln had taken on his way to the White House in 1861. At stops in Baltimore, Harrisburg, Philadelphia, New York City, Albany, Cleveland, Indianapolis, Chicago, and other cities, the crowds that had cheered Lincoln little more than four years earlier gathered to view his body and weep for him. All along the route, people stood in tears by the railroad tracks to watch the funeral train pass.

On May 4, 1865, Lincoln was buried in Oak Ridge Cemetery in Springfield, Illinois. He had come a long way from Hardin County, Kentucky. He had overcome poverty, ignorance, debt, and personal grief to win the nation's highest office. In the face of despair, bitter criticism, and personal threats, he had done what he believed was right for the country, and he had brought it safely through its most dangerous crisis. His place in history was assured. Yet who knows what more he might have gone on to accomplish?

Bibliography

Bruns, Roger. *Abraham Lincoln*. New York: Chelsea House, 1986. This book, although brief, is written for younger readers and covers all major aspects of Lincoln's life. It contains many illustrations.

Duff, John J. *Abraham Lincoln, Prairie Lawyer*. New York: Holt, Rinehart and Winston, 1960. This 433-page book focuses on Lincoln's life in the 1830s and 1840s: how he trained himself in law, formed a successful practice, and defended hundreds of cases. It also paints a vivid picture of 19th-century life in the raw towns of the prairie.

Fehrenbacher, Don E., editor. *Abraham Lincoln: A Documentary Portrait Through His Speeches and Writings*. New York: New American Library, 1964. For those interested in exploring Lincoln's life and thought through his own words, Fehrenbacher's book provides a good general introduction to the speeches and writings of the 16th President.

Freedman, Russell. *Lincoln: A Photobiography*. New York: Clarion Books, 1987. This book won the John Newbery Award for the most distinguished contribution to American literature for children. It is an excellent all-around account of Lincoln, illustrated with nearly 100 photographs of his life and times.

Handlin, Oscar and Lilian. *Abraham Lincoln and the Union*. Boston: Little, Brown, 1980. This short and readable book focuses on Lincoln's struggle to preserve the Union at the outbreak of the Civil War.

Hertz, Emmanuel. *Lincoln Talks: A Biography in Anecdote.* New York: Viking Press, 1939. The author gathered together all the quotations he could find both from Lincoln himself, talking about his life, and from people who knew him. It makes lively reading.

Kunhardt, Dorothy Meserve and Philip B., Jr. *Twenty Days.* New York: Harper & Row, 1965. A "must" for anyone who feels the past come alive through 19th-century photographs and newspaper sketches. This is an illustrated account of Lincoln's assassination and the period of national mourning that followed as his body was carried home to Springfield, Illinois.

Lorant, Stefan. *Lincoln: A Picture History of His Life.* New York: Harper & Row, 1952. This is one of the most thorough photobiographies of Lincoln's life and times. Although it is not as readable as Freedman's book, it contains more illustrations.

Neely, Mark E., Jr. *The Abraham Lincoln Encyclopedia.* New York: McGraw-Hill, 1982. Organized like a one-volume encyclopedia, this book is a handy source of reference material and a good place to look up facts about Lincoln's life and presidency.

Nevins, Allan, editor. *Lincoln and the Gettysburg Address.* Urbana, Illinois: University of Illinois Press, 1964. Everything you wanted to know about the Gettysburg Address can be found in this collection of scholarly essays: how it was written and presented, how it reflects Lincoln's mature philosophy, how it has affected Americans since 1863, and how it compares with other famous speeches.

Oates, Stephen B. *Abraham Lincoln: The Man Behind the Myths.* New York: New American Library, 1985. In this fascinating volume, the author of one of the best Lincoln biographies assembles the vast body of myths, anecdotes, legends, and popular images that have grown up around Lincoln. He examines them for credibility and gives the evidence for and against accepting them as true.

Oates, Stephen B. *With Malice Toward None: The Life of Abraham Lincoln.* New York: New American Library, 1977. Oates is generally recognized as the most thorough and up-to-date of Lincoln's biographers. This volume is lengthy but extremely readable and colorful. Oates covers every phase of Lincoln's life and uses hundreds of quotes from Lincoln and those who knew him to add sparkle to the text.

Sandburg, Carl. *Abraham Lincoln: The Prairie Years and the War Years.* New York: Harcourt, Brace, and World, 1926–1939. Sandburg, one of America's great poets, spent years researching and writing this 6-volume, loving biography. For many years, it was considered the best work on Lincoln's life. Today it has been replaced by newer, more factually complete books, such as those by Stephen Oates. But Sandburg's vivid prose is still exciting and enjoyable, especially in the early sections dealing with Lincoln's frontier childhood.

Thomas, Benjamin P. *Abraham Lincoln: A Biography.* New York: Knopf, 1952. Like Oates' book, this is a fact-filled, one-volume general biography that offers a balanced overview of Lincoln's life.

Williams, Thomas H. *Lincoln and His Generals.* San Francisco: Greenwood Press, 1981. Originally published in 1952, Williams' book is an account of Lincoln's often frustrating relationships with his many Civil War generals and of his struggle to find one who would fight.

Index